out of everywhere

out of

linguistically innovative poetry
by women in North America & the UK

everywhere

edited & introduced by Maggie O'Sullivan

afterword by Wendy Mulford

REALITY STREET EDITIONS
1996

Published by
REALITY STREET EDITIONS
4 Howard Court, Peckham Rye, London SE15 3PH
and
6 Benhall Green, Benhall, Saxmundham, Suffolk IP17 1HU

First edition, 1996

The front cover photograph is by Patricia Crummay
and shows "Water Sculpture" by Paul Burwell
Reproduced with permission

Book design and typesetting by Ken Edwards

Reality Street Editions is grateful to the London Arts Board and
the Eastern Arts Board for making this book possible, in part,
by jointly providing funding

Printed & bound in Great Britain
by BPC Wheatons Ltd, Exeter

A catalogue record for this book is available from the British Library

ISBN: 1-874400-08-3

Acknowledgements

RAE ARMANTROUT: "Crossing" from *Made to Seem* (Sun & Moon, Los Angeles, 1995); "Getting Warm" and "Necromance" from *Necromance* (Sun & Moon, Los Angeles, 1991).

CAROLINE BERGVALL: "Fourth Tableau" from *Strange Passage* (Equipage, Cambridge, 1993).

NICOLE BROSSARD: "Taking it Easy on my Spine" from *Daydream Mechanics*, translated from the French by Larry Shouldice (Coach House Quebec Translations, 1980; first published as *Mécanique jongleuse* by Les Editions de l'Hexagone, Ottawa, 1974); "Igneous Woman, Integral Woman" from *Lovhers,* translated from the French by Barbara Godard (Guernica Editions, Quebec, 1987)(copyright © 1980 by Nicole Brossard and Editions Quinze; translation copyright © 1986 by Barbara Godard and Guernica Editions).

PAULA CLAIRE: ICPA, Oxford, for: "Beebibles" (ICPA No 27, 1990 / cassette ICPA C5, 1991); "Black(w)holewhite(w)hole" (ICPA No 8 / cassette ICPA C3, 1987); "In Vision" (ICPA No 12, 1987; and "Ginkgo Fanfare for the Millennium" 1994 (ICPA No 4, 1985). Writers Forum, London, for: "Jetakeoff" in *Soundsword,* 1972; "High Carbon Steel", 1976. Underwhich Audiographics, Toronto, for: "Jetakeoff", "Beebibles" and "Ginkgo" recorded on Stepping Stones cassette, 1991.

TINA DARRAGH: "adv. fans — the 1968 series" from *adv. fans — the 1968 series* (Leave Books, Buffalo, 1993).

DEANNA FERGUSON: "Sisters of the Even Jesus" appeared in *Raddle Moon* 14 (Vancouver, 1995); "It's Bad for You" in *Mirage 4/Period(ical)* 34 (San Francisco, 1994); "ad ream" is from *The Relative Minor*, Tsunami Editions, Vancouver, 1993.

KATHLEEN FRASER: "understood and scrupulous", "a certain uneven panic" and "girlfriend's wheelchair, gathering combs" from *when new time folds up* (Chax Press, Minneapolis, 1993); "from 'Wing'" from *Wing* (Em Press, 1995).

BARBARA GUEST: "Red Lilies" from *Moscow Mansions* (Viking Press, New York, 1973); "Wild Gardens Overlooked by Night Lights" from *Fair Realism* (Sun & Moon, Los Angeles, 1989); "Winter Horses" from *Defensive Rapture* (Sun & Moon, Los Angeles, 1993).

CARLA HARRYMAN: "from 'Dimblue'" from *In the Mode Of* (Zasterle, Canary Islands, 1991).

LYN HEJINIAN: "from 'My Life (The Nineties)'" was published in *Lingo*; "Chapter 192" from *Oxota: A Short Russian Novel* (The

Figures, Great Barrington, MA, 1991).

FANNY HOWE: "from 'Democracy: Chapters in Verse'" was published in *TriQuarterly*, 1987.

SUSAN HOWE: "from 'A Bibliography of the King's Book or, Eikon Basilike'" from *The Nonconformist's Memorial* (New Directions, New York, 1993).

GRACE LAKE: "Ordered into Quarantine" and "twelve to midnight" from *viola tricolor* (Equipage, Cambridge, 1993); "Silk and Wild Tulips", "the reduction by not first", "by gardenias i cannot telephone", "concilia" and "She Walked where she should have" from *Bernache Nonnette* (Equipage, Cambridge, 1995).

KAREN MAC CORMACK: "Multi-mentional" from *Marine Snow* (ECW Press, Toronto, 1995); "Resex" from *The Tongues Moves Talk* (Chax Press, Minneapolis, 1996); "Paper Sections" was published in *The Capilano Review*.

BERNADETTE MAYER: All work taken from *A Bernadette Mayer Reader* (New Directions, New York, 1992). "From 'Moving'" previously published in *Moving*, 1964; "The Garden" previously published in *Mutual Aid*, 1985; "After Catullus and Horace" previously published in *The Formal Field of Kissing*, 1990.

GERALDINE MONK: "James Device Replies", "Anne Whittle Replies" and "Fox Trot" from *Interregnum* (Creation Books, London, 1994); "The Football Hooligan" and "The Poet" from *Walks in a Daisy Chain* (Magenta, Hebden Bridge, 1991); "Angles" from *Tiger Lilies* (Rivelin Press, Bradford, 1982); "Dragon Fly Howling Monkey" from *Animal Crackers* (Writers Forum, London, 1985); "El Caballo Raptor" from *La Quinta del Sordo* (Writers Forum, 1980).

WENDY MULFORD: "from 'The East Anglian Sequence'" published in *Five Fingers Review* and forthcoming in *The East Anglian Sequence* (Spectacular Diseases, Peterborough, 1996).

MELANIE NEILSON: "from 'Civil Noir'" from *Civil Noir* (Roof Books, New York, 1991).

MAGGIE O'SULLIVAN: "narcotic properties" published in *Avec* and forthcoming in *Palace of Reptiles* (Sun & Moon, Los Angeles); "Hill Figures" and "Garb" from *In the House of the Shaman* (Reality Street Editions, London & Cambridge, 1993); "A Lesson from the Cockerel" and "Second Lesson from the Cockerel" from *Unofficial Word* (Galloping Dog Press, Newcastle upon Tyne, 1988).

CARLYLE REEDY: "3 floorplan texts" published in *words worth magazine*, Yeovil, 1994.

JOAN RETALLACK: "from AFTERRIMAGES" from *AFTERRIMAGES* (Wesleyan University Press, University Press of New England,

Hanover & London, 1995).

DENISE RILEY: "*Lure, 1963*", "So Is It?", "Oleanna", "Rayon", "Song", "Poem beginning with a line from Proverbs" from *Mop Mop Georgette* (Reality Street Editions, London & Cambridge, 1993).

LISA ROBERTSON: "from 'Debbie: an epic'" published in *Parataxis* (Sussex) and also in *Exact Change Yearbook* (1995).

LESLIE SCALAPINO: "from 'New Time'" published in *Chelsea* magazine (New York).

CATRIONA STRANG: "from 'Low Fancy'" from *Low Fancy* (ECW Press, Toronto, 1993).

FIONA TEMPLETON's texts are previously unpublished.

ROSMARIE WALDROP: "The Attraction of the Ground" and "from 'The Perplexing Habit of Falling'" from *Lawn of Excluded Middle* (Tender Buttons, Providence, 1993).

DIANE WARD: "Cartographies" published in *Ribot* and *Tailspin;* "from 'Look at Joseph Cornell'" in *self • evidence* (catalogue for exhibition at Los Angeles Contemporary Exhibitions) and also in *Exhibition* (Potes & Poets, Connecticut, 1995) and *World Ceiling* (Roof Books, New York, 1995).

MARJORIE WELISH: "Twenty-three Modern Stories" from *Casting Sequences* (University of Gerogia Press, Athens, Georgia & London, 1993); "Crude Misunderstandings" and "Opera" published in *New American Writing* 11 (Chicago, 1993); "Macbeth in Battle" published in *Parataxis* (Sussex).

HANNAH WEINER: "from 'silent teachers'" from *Silent Teachers Remembered Sequel* (Tender Buttons, Providence, 1993).

Where no acknowledgement is given, a poem can be assumed to be previously unpublished. Not all instances of magazine publication are cited.

Contents

To the Reader

IN THE summer of 1994 Ken Edwards and Wendy Mulford of Reality Street Editions invited me to edit a proposed anthology of contemporary linguistically innovative poetry by women in the US, Canada and the UK. Here it is then: *Out of Everywhere.*

The title is lifted from an edited transcript of a discussion following Rosmarie Waldrop's talk "Alarms and Excursions" given in full in Charles Bernstein's indispensable *The Politics of Poetic Form* (Roof Books, 1990), where an unidentified audience member puts the question

> But I imagine that you must have some difficulty with the more explicit, politically engaged writing, don't you? Or with the exclusion of poets like yourself and Susan Howe, or say Lorine Niedecker, from, for example, the Gilbert and Gubar anthology of women's writing? There's an extra difficulty being a woman poet and writing the kind of poetry you write: you are out of everywhere [laughter].
>
> WALDROP: I take that as a compliment. I've more or less claimed this is the position of poetry.

I hope this collection will suggest the extraordinary range and diversity and also demonstrate that much of the most challenging, formally progressive and significant work over recent years, particularly, in the US (a fact acknowledged by my inclusion of a large percentage of US poets) is being made by women.

Each poet featured here (to paraphrase Ulla Dydo, in her magnificent *A Gertrude Stein Reader,* Northwestern University Press, 1993) does not *represent* a familiar world and therefore cannot be read in familiar ways. Consequently, many of them, through brave insistence and engagement in explorative, formally progressive language practices, find themselves excluded from conventional, explicitly generically committed or thematic anthologies of women's poetry. Excluded from "women's canons", such work does, however, connect up with linguistically innovative work by men who have themselves also transcended the agenda-based and cliché-ridden rallying positions of mainstream poetry. Rather than perpetuating prevalent notions of writing poems "about" something, the poets here, to my mind, have each in their own imaginative way committed themselves to excavating *language* in all its multiple voices and tongues, known and unknown.

Historically, such pioneering poets as Gertrude Stein, Mina Loy, HD and Lorine Niedecker have done much to shape an energetic and influential, though marginalised tradition of innovative writing practices. The poets in this compilation are contributing to expanding the horizons of this practice. All of them work in English, with the exception of French-Canadian Nicole Brossard, included as a collation such as this would be inconceivable without her pioneering work, thankfully available for us in English translation.

Many of these poets are involved in long poetic sequences or in project-orientated work, the textual, aesthetic and political perspectives of which can only be glimpsed here. This engagement with larger poetic discourses and practices embraces inter- and multi-media work and performative directions and celebrates poetry as event. Furthermore, a large number of the poets here are active in production as magazine and poetry press editors and publishers. These include: Paula Claire, International Concrete Poetry Archive (ICPA); Deanna Ferguson, *BOO* magazine and co-publisher of Tsunami Editions; Lyn Hejinian, Tuumba Press and co-editor and publisher (with Barrett Watten) of *Poetics Journal*; Wendy Mulford, Street Editions/Reality Street Editions; Melanie Neilson, co-editor (with Jessica Grim) of *Big Allis* magazine; Lisa Robertson/Catriona Strang, co-editors (with Susan Clark) of *Raddle Moon*; Leslie Scalapino, O Books (a poetry press with more than 30 titles); Diane Ward, co-editor (with Phyllis Rosenzweig) of *Primary Writing* broadsheet; and my own Magenta Press. Some have been active over many years, such as Kathleen Fraser with *HOW(ever)* magazine and Rosmarie and Keith Waldrop's Burning Deck, soon to celebrate over 35 years of independent publishing.

If you are a general poetry reader, unfamiliar with a good many of these poets, I passionately hope that this collection, the first of its kind, will inspire you to further seek their work, and those of others too (which space limitations prohibit me from including), who I believe are among the most adventurous, intellectually challenging and imaginative of our times.

Bon voyage.

Maggie O'Sullivan, November 1995

Susan Howe

from: A Bibliography of the King's Book
or, Eikon Basilike

ΕΙΚΩΝ ΒΑΣΙΛΙΚΗ.

Bradshaw went on in a long harangue misapplying Law and History

Wall I

Language of state secrets

Brazen

The pretended Court
of Justice
_____

Upon the picture of His Majesty sitting in his Chair | before

Grave

the High Court of Injustice
_____

and

Small trespas to misprison

Prison

now nonexistent dramatis personae
confront each
other

between

Heroic Virtue & Fame

Steps

ENGELANDTS MEMORIAEL

Tragicum Theatrum Actorum

Similar (not identical)

unsigned portraits of

Laud Charles I Fairfax

Holland Hamilton Capel

Cromwell

Ordinance

crucified by that sea of blood

The malicious author or instigator

Tract the treasons

throw down

Always causes set down

Forts Navy Militia

of Joy

O make me

Some passages

thrown on this person

for a different message

an intellectualist

Was taken

A
P
l
o
t
v
o

The People Contemporary History

Through the populacy

Through populacy

in a low voice

two or three words

He bowed down his head and said

they kept

past

that I hide Security and their

Security

strive against starry scruples

at times at times

and wall   the brazen wall

I am weary of life

Pretend Justice to cover Perjury

P
r
i   s
s between o
e   n
t
s

The sentiment sentiment
Goes peers ferrets to the last

Obligation

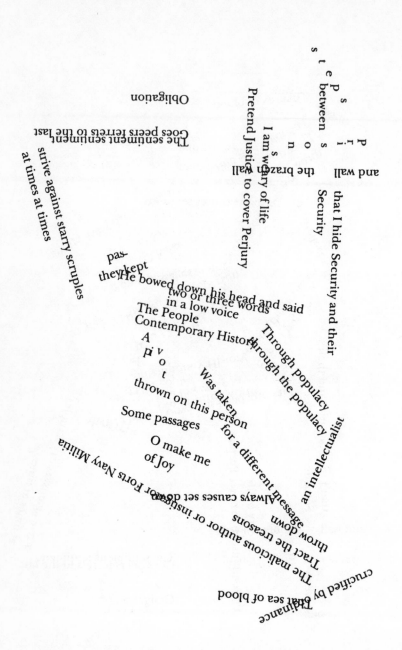

P
r
i
s
o
n
s

s t e p s
between

Pretend Justice to cover Perjury
I am weary of life
the brazen wall

P
and wall
that I hide Security and their
Security

Obligation

The sentiment sentiment
Goes peers ferries to the last

strive against starry scruples
at times at times

pas-
they kept
He bowed down his head and said
two or three words
in a low voice
The People
Contemporary History

Through populacy
through the populacy
an intellectualist

A
p
i
v
o
t

Was taken
thrown on this person
for a different message

Some passages

O make me
of Joy

Always causes set down
throw down
Tract the reasons
The malicious author or instead Forts Navy Militia
crucified by

Trajinance
Vast sea of blood

Finding the way full of People
Who had placed themselves upon the Theatre
To behold the Tragedy
He desired he might have *Room*
Speech came from his mouth   to the right
Historiography of open fields   Signed . King in profile

Mend the Printers faults
The place name and field name
as thou doest them espy
Centuries of compulsion and forced holding
For the Author lies in Gaol   All the Civil War Authorities

and knows not why

A cleric's forgery
of a pseudo-biographical
apology

England's Black Tribunal : Containing The Complete
Tryal of King CHARLES the First by the pretended
High Court of Justice in *Westminster-Hall*, begun *Jan.*
20, 1648. Together with his Majesty's Speech on the
Scaffold, erected at *Whitehall-Gate*, on Tuesday *Jan.* 30,
1648.   It passed with the Negative.

                                    they kept prisoner

An intellectualist or... some subjective telling love

He bowed down his head and said
in a low voice
two or three words
The People
Contemporary History
Through popular
through the popular
intellectualist
A
p
i
v
o
t
Was taken
this person
thrown on...for a different message
Some passages
O make me
of Joy

Dr. Juxon.   There is but one Stage more, this Stage is

turbulent and troublesome, it is a short one;

but you may consider, it will soon carry you a very great

Way: It will carry you from Earth to Heaven, and there

you shall find a great deal of cordial Joy and Comfort.

King.   I go from a corruptible to an incorruptible

Crown, where no Disturbance can be, no Distur-

bance in the World

This still house

An unbeaten way

My self and words

The King kneeling

Old raggs about him

All those apopthegems

Civil and Sacred

torn among fragments

Emblems gold and lead

Must lie outside the house

Side of space I must cross

To write against the Ghost

Joan Retallack

from: AFTERRIMAGES

Afterrimages in what follows were determined by chance procedures.

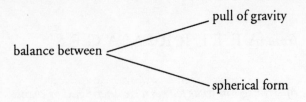

covering of short hairs or fur

something on or near the surface

i.e.specificcrystallineformoftaxonomiccategories

....

So reulith hire hir hertes gost withinne,
That though she bende, yeet she stant on roote

_____

                              rs o

                  ne   th su

              orm   onomi   ate

        .. ..

            e hir hert

this was morning

deep in her body

delicious asymmetry of sight and sound

sourire jaune's yellow smile

scenes of translation

defies translation

Saph [...]gment

(now she shines among Lyd....worn............)?

---

od

gh an

ne

e   lat

ns   io

vol low on radio • in Tangier

no smoke but smell of alarm

(see a pre-Socratic on fire in the mind)

nice being out here in the sun

(or St. Augustine on time)

$\pm$o = no future tense in dreams = o$\pm$

(poetry eludes genre as well)

sage of ectopic eye

logical series of unsolicited occasions

(see   i   in   e

          in   e   in

                              o

                         ᵗ ʷ

               ec

          s

need to give latitude which is often silence and/or

Virginia said she likes the word *breach*

whydon'tfliesdielikeflies

[........To speke of wo that is in mariage..........
Men may devyne and glosen up and doun
But wel I woot expres withoute lye]

142

........] all this I see
........]plainly] now

at this point Paul

mentioned that

sunbeams are

extracted from
cucumbers in
Gulliver's Travels

....] all th

oint P

nb

everyone was puzzled how
11 native speakers could
get into so much trouble

still later Calvino's sixth memo it

still later it they it

the in in the vernacular out of inferno theory

in the late 18th century they in the Cornish language it became
   (extinct)
it could no still later it no longer could be it that it was said they
later still to get the in out of integrity it too

∴ (dissyllable throughout) ∴

Terra pestem teneto : salus hic maneto.   DLHR, p.58

-charm for foot pain-

[*word foot* defined as
word containing at least
one strong (acute) stress]

[here the logic seems clear]

but
the lear in clear
the ear in lear
the a in ear
the in
the

(This is this meant to explain Ptolemy's "Handy Tables"
with naked torsos gesticulating in little niches atop each
column of text.)
Is *this* the anatomy of melancholy?
Does seeing imply distance?

poet o the Land-O-Lakes District

      Spitting Imagists

Lord and Lady Elgin and their watches

hard   dry   and   photo   phobic

terrorists burning toast (*boast?*) in Winnipeg

                  perhaps thi
                     the
                        ing of

---

poet   -O

sti?)

Tina Darragh

adv. fans – the 1968 series

for Hannah Weiner and Mimi Darragh

"Among the problems are these: What kinds of cognitive structures are developed by humans on the basis of their experience, specifically, in the case of acquisition of language?"

Chomsky, *Reflections on Language*, page 137

I read the sign "adv. fans →" as "adverb fans this way", rather than the other possible interpretations of that abbreviation

"ad valorem fans this way" or
"advance fans this way" or
"adverse fans this way" or
"advertisement fans this way"

the last being the sign's intent — a public library display of old "advertising fans" ripped so that words from other fans and/or the display's backdrop showed through. At the time, I was trying to figure out if a poem could be in the form of a theatre with words/sounds in every seat. The image in my mind was a Hannah Weiner performance in DC in the early '80s in which voices arose from the audience in conjunction with Hannah reading alone on stage. I wanted to "build" a poem based on my memory of that reading, avoiding both the "naturalization" and stigmatization of multiple, overlapping voices.

When I first saw the window full of "adv. fans", I thought of knotted hands opening ("Here's the church, here's the steeple, open the door and see the people") and intermingling voices. The fan's folds were the rows of seats; the voice, center-stage, a hand opening and closing.

A concurrent desire was to investigate what went wrong with language in 1968. I remembered the dissolution of alternative living arrangements and businesses as beginning with words — the failure of political projects as being partly a language problem. I started to collect words/expressions first used in 1968 after a documentary on the '60s included a right-wing strategist proclaiming that, after the Left's speeches at the Democratic National Convention, "they knew they had us".

The "adv. fan" steps are:

1) Photocopy pages from one or more dictionaries (using different ones can help in the transcriptions).
2) Randomly tear one dictionary page and then paste it over a whole one.
3) Fold into a fan and read.
4) Transcribe a section and place between two definitions attributed to having first been said in 1968.

voice1 — over the phone:

"I'm going to come over there and lick some little pussy, and there's nothing you can do about it."

on the playground afterwards:

"He signs our paychecks &
we're all living paycheck to paycheck
& what *can* we do about it?"

---

voice2— the warm hand

I want the warm hand
the warm hand doesn't call me by name
I want _____

_____ is wrong
the warm hand is screaming

YOU want finger pointing
YOU want fingers close up
YOU pounding-no *YOU* pounding-go
YOU pounding-never

_____ goes away

1968 — "survivor syndrome" — defined as a set of clinical characteristics exhibited by someone subjected to terror during a military action.

1968 — "survivor" and "W.A.R." (World of Abnormal Rearing) are incorporated into family therapy terminology regarding domestic violence.

1971 — use of term "survivor" in literature to describe anyone who addresses adversity.

1991 — *The Reader's Guide to Popular Literature* lists 258 instances of "survivor" in article titles.

"survivors" — as formerly occupied territories
who have been set free
and by virtue of invasion
are owed _____
due eventually

survivor-pedestal
one voice that oversees:
"We are where the words ferred
when the warm fist made them flee."

What, if anything happens to the present tense when language acquisition and corporal punishment occur simultaneously?

The expression I associate with the dissolution of communal or alternative living experiences circa 1968 is "I'm a *survivor*". The problem at hand would be one of generic territoriality (regarding such things as toilet paper or milk), secondary to a general inequality based on earning capacity and worldly status. A slight of milk would evoke a "survivor" statement, a seemingly melodramatic response but one which indicated that all future negotiations already had been settled in favor of those who were actively experiencing pain — the uniform code of trauma. The difficult issues of the economic differences of those living there and their effect on slice-of-life inequalities couldn't be addressed. The living experiments failed. For lack of long-term financial backing, the political experiments were of such short duration that our arguments regarding why they failed are based more on conjecture than observation.

My sister Mimi works in an "employment program" for the "mentally ill". One of the members often would pace, his hands up to his temples, opening and closing his fists, his fingers so many exclamation points in the air. Mim would ask "What are the voices saying?" He'd reply: "It's the class struggle going on in here."

---

dicker suit
riage control
iof also me
to priate

---

one voice needed for daily functioning, multipile voices needed to change our functioning

layer hand over fist
opens fist under hand
f and h st f an fan

shot line - 1968, A.P. Bolder. *Compl. Man Skin Diving*. xiii 248.
A shot line...should be used from a boat when diving in bad visibility.

stal
gyla
ficia
al   2.

flat-topped iceberg

Also,
[<
copal]
rmor tasset.

clasp. Also, **tach.**

Survey, tachym-

tacheos, gen.

quality of being reserved
2. *Sco   Law*, a form
thro **efec** unduly long
(GIMCR   *taciturni*
1. the thir   *taciturn*
bet. 2. the   *tes), n.*
by this letter
gimel, lit., camel ur -c 12
n. 1. a sm
end an
with a **ktai** broad he

tele-player - 1968. *Daily Telegraph.* 12 Dec 25/3.
The tele-player will cost about 200 and each tele-cartridge... 20.

teletransport - 1968, *Punch*, 2 Oct. 488/1.
A Royal Martian Vole...teletransported herself to your planet in 1964.

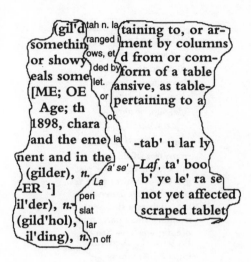

shopper - 1968, H.C. Rae. *Few Small Bones.* II. v. 113.
He bought enough tinned food...then lugging the laden shopper, set out along
the main street.

ASH - 1968, *Christian Science Monitor*, 1/30, 5.
Most recently there is the formation of the brand new Action on Smoking
and Health (ASH) to act as a legal arm of the antismoking forces.

---

an *feluc(c)a*, from obsole
p ed or fined rath sev a p
r doesn't presen lly
6. to go about on t
as a ghost: *to beli* s
tool, pointer, or p
de, slip, or move m
r the like: A uces
or or *hen yo* riate to
members of this sex. 4.
an organ, such as a pist
g seeds or spores after fe
mens: *female flowers.*
art, such as a slot or r
mentary male part, such
ninate; weak. -- See
F., fem. 1. A membe
ing. 2. Anything pon
distinguished fro s by
nly pistillate flo o walk
lkrd ou

---

hostess apron - 1968, *Wanganui (N.Z.) Chronical*, 15 Nov. 8/3.
(winner of competition) Hostess apron: Mrs. S. 1, Mrs. A.J.M. 2.

Paula Claire

JETAKEOFF

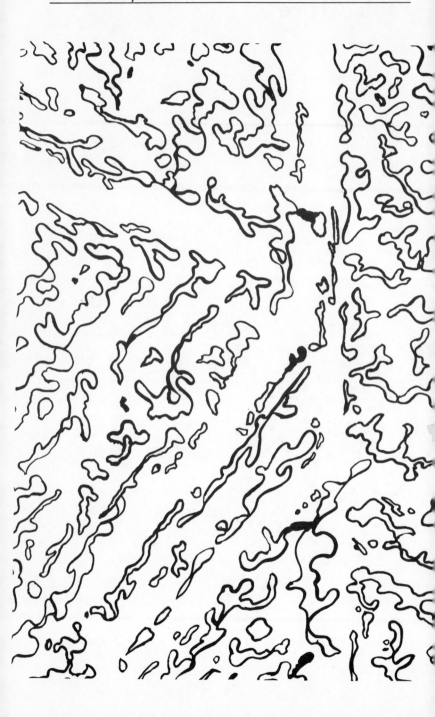

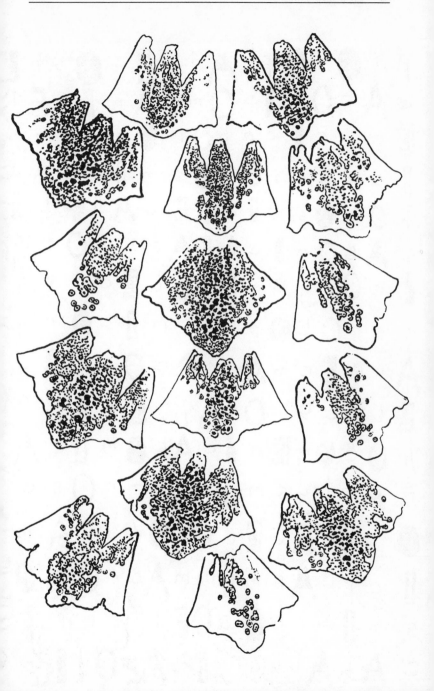

p r o t o p l A s m I c o s m I
c A T o m I c O r g A n I c E L
E c t r I c p h O t o g r A p h
E c m I c r O c o s m I c m A c
r O c o s m I c m E T A b o l I
c A t o m I c A T A s t r o p h
I c O r g A n I c E L E c t r I
c p r o t o p l A s m I c o r g
A s m I c m A c r o c O s m I c
E L E c t r O M A g n E t I c p
h O t o g E n I c A t o m I c A
t A c l y s m I c m I c r O s c
● p I c E L E c t r o d y n A m
I c p l A s m I c m A c r O c
s m I c p h O t O E L E c t r I
c A T A l y s t I c A t o m I c

GO HEAVENLY GUEST ETHEREAL MESSENGER

etherealight

etherealight

etherealight

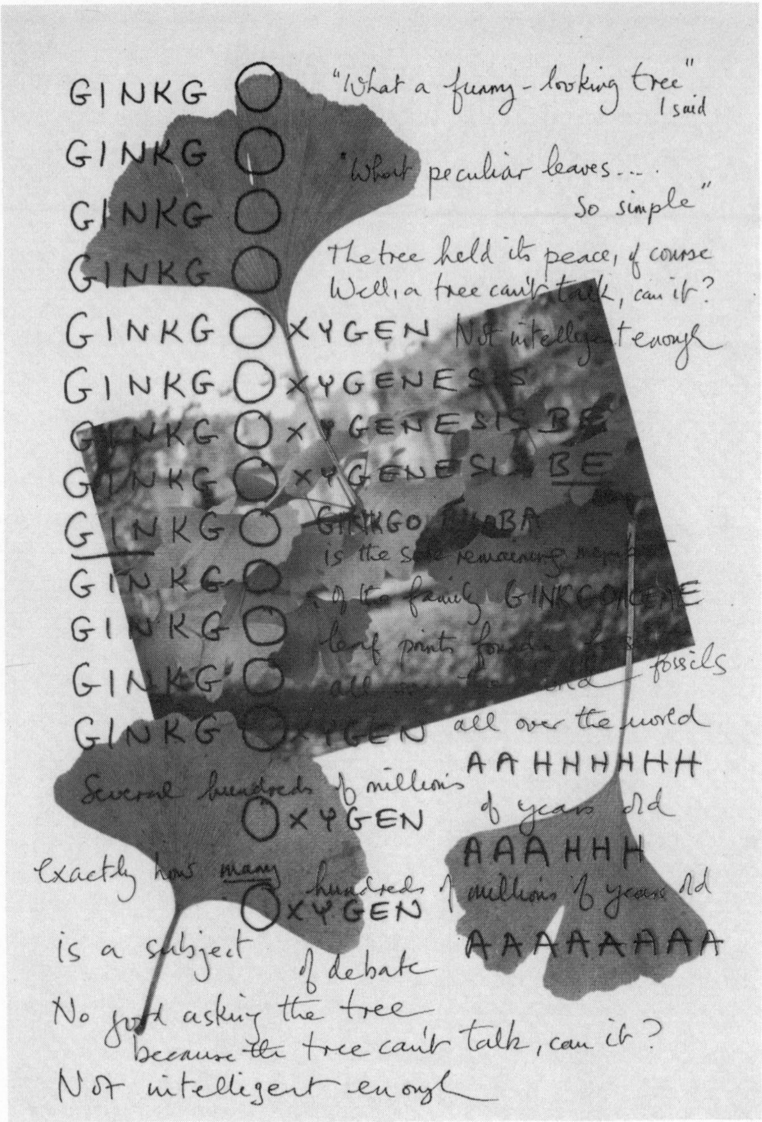
GINKG O
"What a funny-looking tree" I said
GINKG O
"What peculiar leaves...
So simple"
GINKG O
GINKG O
The tree held its peace, of course
Well, a tree can't talk, can it?
GINKG OXYGEN
Not intelligent enough
GINKG OXYGENES
GINKG OXYGENESIS BE
GINKG OXYGENESIS BE
GINKG O
GINKG O
GINKG O
GINKG O
fossils
GINKG OXYGEN
all over the world
AAHHHHHH
Several hundreds of millions
of years old
OXYGEN
AAAHHH
Exactly how many hundreds of millions of years old
OXYGEN
AAAAAAA
is a subject of debate
No good asking the tree
because the tree can't talk, can it?
Not intelligent enough

1. JETAKEOFF 1970

Typewriter text reworked from a "part Mobile Poem" 28.1.69. This poem can be relied upon to grab the attention of the audience, especially in schools. The text is performed by me, with improvisation, from the bottom upwards as far as the words in capital letters, accompanied by an increasingly loud hum from the audience. Then they shout out the words in capitals, making maximum noise in "R O A R A O R". I then perform the diagonal line of text, my voice rising to its highest pitch, looking skywards with arm raised and finger pointing to the disappearing plane. I designed this text as a large-scale permutational neon poem in red and blue, for an airport wall. First performance: St Martin's School of Art, London, 1970.

2. HIGH CARBON STEEL 1974

From a set of 9 tracings of photomicrographs, their patterns perceived as elementary codes, a rudimentary language: therefore performable improvisation texts for voices and instruments. This an electron photomicrograph x 25,000. First performance: Bob Cobbing's Experimental Poetry Workshop, The Poetry Society, Earl's Court Square, London, 1975.

3. BEEBIBLES 1981

Tracings of 15 split-open foxgloves, revealing the unique coded messages inside each one, privy only to the bees. For the 15th Anniversary of the Association of Little Presses. First performance using actual foxgloves at Gilbert Adair's *Subvoicive* reading series, Highgate Community Centre, London, July, 1981.

4. BLACK(W)HOLEWHITE(W)HOLE 1986

A page of handwritten performance poem from PHOS PHOR, an evening's participatory entertainment: a mixture of recitative, chant, song, and sound poetry, with symbolic actions: to increase cosmic awareness. Created for first performance with Steven Paxton and musicians from Texas Tech University at New Music America / The Houston Festival, April 1986, held in the Music Department Concert Hall, University of Houston, USA.

5. IN VISION 1986

A page from a set of 16 "text-iles", a development of the 5 typewriter "text-iles" from ETHEREALIGHT, 1984: acetates made from these and overlaid to create ever more complex effects: to be viewed stereoscopically. Improvisation texts for voices and instruments. For exhibition at the First International Festival of Living Poetry, Figuera da Foz, Portugal, January 1987, curator Fernando Aguiar.

6. GINKGO FANFARE FOR THE MILLENNIUM 1994

Chant (with processional walk) forming the climax to the last of a proposed set of 7 Schemes to celebrate the Millennium: the planting of 2001 Ginkgo trees by the year 2001AD; to be situated in various localities in GB. Each site to be inaugurated with words, music, walking and picnics. Developed from an ongoing devotion to the Ginkgo tree, begun in 1984/5 with a performance poem, July 1985. First performance: Real Art Ways, Hartford, CT USA, with the Paxton Group musicians/electronics, November 1985.

Diane Ward

I am within action without activity, my attraction to wrap myself permanent and apart to sling myself from myself, a center point. I am pressed. I am tied earthward with hideous ribbons, control operating to extract the operation from mechanization. We squirm, here, back to consciousness, punctuate. I am filled in with social motion, a twist toward yours in your direction. I am pitching through recurring periods toward you. Drop here? Cram gestures drawn with broad regional fantasies. I see chaos in

HEIR TO PHYSICAL LABOR (tender and growing in groups or masses

Sure I'd made a portal, some kind of evidence of my awe. Halfway opening the valve of public peace and assurance. Awe. Using both feet in a habitual manner: conformity and precaution crush. We began as movable barriers in a system of arrangement. Secure but with twitches. Restrained misgiving. Cognizant of purpose, space omitted in conversation.

my spare self made-to-droop, arms circulating between currents of pre-seized views of self combinations along and additional, further — a lowering voice blocked ambient ... — b... ...re, ...ality, gunsho... set check ...cefully upon playing roles with rr without ?... F'pon—I thi'D ...ody uni: REMᴏʳIN I N G

taking the
definition into
me: <u>no</u> is to
r e n d e r
separate, flow

taking the
definition into
me: <u>no</u> is to
r e n d e r
separate, flow

taking the
definition into
me: <u>no</u> is to
r e n d e r
separate, flow

taking the
definition into
me: <u>no</u> is to
r e n d e r
separate, flow

taking the
definition into
me: <u>no</u> is to
r e n d e r
separate, flow

taking the
definition into
me: <u>no</u> is to
r e n d e r
separate, flow

taking the
definition into
me: <u>no</u> is to
r e n d e r
separate, flow

taking the
definition into
me: <u>no</u> is to
r e n d e r
separate, flow

taking the
definition into
me: <u>no</u> is to
r e n d e r
separate, flow

taking the
definition into
me: <u>no</u> is to
r e n d e r
separate, flow

comfort is
pushed apart —
waiting in a
motionful
state — he's
nervous,
collecting
issues to keep
him from
flatter
scrutiny — are
we together
here — I wound
part of my
self, my ball.
more tightly —
reductions in
flight two
points merging
so tightly,
there seems to
be, seems to
be a spot that
could receive
the hand when
it lights —

...out location — a geometric surface (my) pl(f)ace transform(ed) a spherical present — ease of movement between tips met roughly halfway between linear represent ation of eye(las)he (is the seen — a sphere floating in socket "a window" and behind glass, plan only of speech figured through line

437 United States

internalized
layer,
manifest cloud
destinations,
as if I had
only
combinations
of adjectives,
on my word
able to
measure
contentment

ternalized
stinations, as if I had
mbinations of adjectives, on
'd able to measure contentment

cloud
destinati
ons, as
if I had
only
combinati
ons of
adjective
s, on my
word
t

manifest cloud
destinations, as if I had only
on my
word able
to
measure
co

manifest cloud
internalized layer, manifest cloud
destinations, as if I had only, on r
nations of adjectives, or
asure contentment

ons
adjectiv
s, on my
word able
to
measure
co

est
nd
destinati
ons, as
if I had
only
combinati
ons of
adjective
s, on my
ord able

as of
adjective
s, on my
word able
to
measure
contentme

layer, manifest cloud

internalize
destinations, as if I had only
combinations of adjectives, or
word able to measure conten

from: Look at Joseph Cornell

I want to tell you about my world:

First the crossbars: rigid and straight, parallel the earth mimicking the symbol of horizon violently speckled into shades of blue.

The flowers are dead and dried a cracking brown.

White figure of the world is death, fierce innocence and sentimentality.

The darkest uprights, beyond my mind's blackness, are held apart by brown.

The ivory figure/black figure are symbols of themselves and the objects they tread upon.

The blue ground is interrupted by white spots of paint or else. The blue ground is solid but reflecting white spots of light or else.

The hunter is a halftone, raising rifle high onto his right shoulder. He aims at another and is within the other's range.

The brown box is a coffin. The blue paint a joke, constraint.

The clown's huge and heavy hands are immobile as his clothes fade completely to white. Diamond jester print splatters all around the walls.

There is no purchasable commodity that can stop this.
I'm going to burst into 6 panels of perfectly circular
shattered by-product.

Then carefully reconstruct the shape of a window from
what's left of the world.

In the twilight it's blue. Blue is a figure gazing
longingly toward its object that gazes longingly away.

The yardstick of my fantasy life is constructed of the 9
to 5 fabric and marked along its extension by words of
denial and encouragement.

If you can't, I never did and will never feel it either.

This heritage where my miters don't meet.

Carla Harryman

from: Dimblue

After Theresa Hak Kyung Cha's **Dictée**

The arrogance of the contemporary in relationship to the contemporary. Water. A soft relationship. Entrance. Contemporary. It. Breaking. Summons. Nor waters. Contemporary. Summons arrogance. Breaks. Not water. History. Waters. It makes it name itself contemporary. He. No, he. It. Who leaves. The ground. First. Contemporaneous water. Somebody says, "The first time." Is the only time. Speaking it. Is water. She. Or education. Preference. That mattered was not the same thing. Could not literate. Therefore could not contemporary. It being written history speaking. And one mind could not exchange for another mind only history. Says water meaning education. She is education history. It is contemporary. Preferring history. Not water. The first water. The only summons. It is written education waters. Does delicious silence hear delicious silence written? Child? Water? History? As speaking child. And water. Written water and arrogance. Not as a plant. But leaves and water he it or she. Leaving history to the contemporary. Taken as history. As child taken to be plant.

Breaking slip. Is education. The contemporaneous oversight. Blue for cool. Water for cool. Yellow for speech. Having a contemporary absence. A literate water. Yellow for speech. He naming itself delicious. Forgetting. The first time is the only time slipping.

It is she. It is she again. It is preference. Words in the mind on the ground speaking not writing but history in the air. Yellow. For blue. And yellow. For blue as blue speaking. The first association was arrogance. History and arrogance. Contemporaneity and oversight. Paring of blue and yellow. Slivers of preference and literate. As written history might keep. The cool oversight whose soft leaves water. And later breaking. Slips.

Brazil. There is no blue the first time. There is no blue the second time. There is blue where blue came from. Arrogance written with desire. Desire being not water. But he. Only once. As a plant taken to be history. But blue. Where blue came from. This is a lament. If you want history go east. Preference. Lament. Plant. Delicious. Literate. Slip. Not history but slip. Finally not negation but slip. Water. She. As child's historical oversight. Is the only time. Speaking. Later. Plants. Where word plants speaking but not education. Which is Brazil. Or preference planting negative. So grows the delicious history going east then where blue came from. Secondly as slip. As Brazil. As child taken to be plant. Therefore preference. And anti. She is education history. She. Is water written lament. And cool education written blue. A literate blue. A literate yellow. And arrogance she. Speaks. Forgetting. The first Brazil. Is yellow and so speaking yellow as blue as writing. Lament. Yellow and blue. Slip. The negative. Bury the negative. Growing written water. And arrogance. But first. The oversight.

Dim. I have not caught up. It is the rest that counts historically speaking. Therefore. Trees round the pond. It is a convenience. Nevertheless. An abandoned negative. But first the oversight.

So the experiment was he. Rounding the pond. Trees literate as child's history. Adhered to rather than abandoned. And so speaking but not about what he saw. The words immersed. In rounding the pond.

It is visible but it is not a tree. The negative that makes of a word material comes from the language making capacity and music. Trees music language co-exist. With the comings and goings the dim. She is not the same nor he. But without a negative he and she. Writing he and she co-exist. Immersion and water separate. And co-author the experiment. If history accounted for made accounts of was literate on the person at rest in opposition to or not even in opposition to action then a group of ideas related to non-action would change the nature of need. So that one would say, "I need to act." And not, "I need to rest." The rest would challenge the power base. And the literate she. She. And he. He. Forget the first Brazil. There is no blue as history. The negative is still going east and has not dispensed with activity. Trees music language co-exist in a rumble. The pond also rumbles. Rounding education. As a plant taken to be water. Then child. Moving from one preference to another as if it were experimental. An electronic negative writes to non-action. Dear Sugar. Is literate child. Taken to be history.

War machines round the pond. He she and he he and she she rest. There are no provactuers in the language of rest and the machines round unprovoked.

A sinister sexuality preferring history. It makes it name itself contemporary. Blue where blue came from. As not break or plant. But lining pond rounding rest. Therefore only in one place. Written. But not literate. Taken to be history as child.

It is a lie that it has gotten worse. And it is a lie that it has gotten better. It is the same. Rounding the desert is the same as rounding the pond. No one is there but rounding but lining. If history were made by a series resting. Yet there are many arguments for the contrary. Although voices disappear as fast as the contemporary arrogance taken as history can obliterate them. Though music contradicts. She. She. He. He. The child sings. And contradicts. She brings preference to history. Banishes contemporary. Banishes pond and trees with people rounding and lining pond and trees. She imposes a meaning on people that negates the beauty of rounding and lining pond and trees.

Lyn Hejinian

from: A Border Comedy

Book Two

Imposed and above
And under a tree in the park is an infant on its
      back gazing at the sky
Whose many points of acute and autonomous blue are
      shimmering
Free of chronology and awaiting the right words
To exercise an enormous influence
The nameless object
Repeating the nameless object of this speculation
Which has its antecedents in the sky at night
And in uneven numbers
But it can never feel entirely sure that it will be
      understood
Since this is meaningless without a context
To complete the metamorphoses into pleasure
Of the many modifications which the infant will make
      so as not to overpower everything
With fate
Fate is just a form of censorship
A lowering of the volume of clouds
So that the infant is obscured, its first words
Lost:
[Something, something...] *gone* [*wrong?*]
[Labial sounds, then] *horizontal pins of crickets*
[Feedback, babbling...] *ape ear* [or, possibly, *a*
      pear] *all along* [*all alone?*]
[Cooing...] *points in the air*
Staring back at the next censor
In the next century already drawing a picture of
      itself
As something incompletely lost

In a future stirring empathy, creating news of
    itself
Fate diminishes expectations
But this attention to ethics doubles my enthusiasm
By admitting wilfulness (with its many digressions)
And where strength isn't enough, one has to resort
    to invention
To points standing on the ocean or an anecdotalist
    in a tree
Pursuing adventures in the great detail we see
Can we say that anecdotalists are provocateurs?
Anecdotalists on wings?
They are of consequence and of extremes
Making appearances as quasi-characters whose quasi-
    plot ends with the telling of a story
In which the question *why?* throws everything into
    chaos
By requiring retelling
In one sentence
Another smaller
Blown up
Enormously depicted though in the background
Like music for "A Tale of Bygone Years" or "The
    History of a Terrible Vengeance"
Or any scene with obscure horizons—
Maria (looking out the window): What kind of bird is
    that, a blue jay? It just flew by
Colonel (kissing her shoulder, his back to the
    window): A blue jay
So we can't see the transfer,
The whole word
I think perhaps it will not require capitulation but
    only my naked self
Moving forward
'There,' 'outside,'
But that isn't experience until it's formed,
Falling before dark
The anecdotalist feeling it a duty to make the story

understood
Watching the sunset as that sunset, not as any other
Returning
Flying
And very ordinarily
Ovid says, being a bird is not the worst of all
        fates
The small bird chases the larger across the park
The power and activity of both should be enough
But they're characteristic
I grab a bush, see mice gnawing at its roots,
And reach my tongue to the drops of honey on its
        leaves
As in a tale
Once there was a girl who could ride birds
High or low, she looked everywhere
But the mystery remained
The sky was as swift and narrow as a river and the
        glints flashing from its depths changed from
        pink to green and then to yellow
How sad!
'Thoughts' and 'things' are names for two different
        sorts of objects
Which common sense doesn't always contrast
The the mockingbird's song will be muffled by the
        wail of the fire siren
And both will fade away
But after all the thought remains
And contributes to the chaos that good stories
        introduce
Scene: I am stepping forward with one foot lifted to
        cross over a creek when I suddenly pull it
        back, deciding, for no apparent reason, to stay
        on this side
But the transfer of meaning from one word to the
        next will proceed nonetheless
Until the bird burns the river to gravel
Meanwhile I'll remain in two places at once

Often
That and this
With board to water
Hardly knowing what I want
To beat the current?
To cross and see what's waiting on the other side
Juxtaposed and progressing?
And myself telling?
I see a luminous blue cave and dogs dashing from it
Imploring
Through unrepresentative light
Through ice light
Until the ice goes out from under them and they fall
       through
But a lot of things have changed
An anecdotal story is merely a span
Consisting of separate facts
Each tenuously connected to the next
Where what we respond to are the attractiveness of
       the facts
And the view each one provides
There are even such things as philosophical
       anecdotes
Going around
Beautifully feathered and perfectly circling
So as not to diverge even an inch from the truths
Thrown among things
And lost in the woods
Then along came a woodcutter wearing blue boots
And carrying a sapling in a sack over his shoulder
To justify his claims
To the accuracy of the metaphors of branching,
       flight, and perching
He uses
To describe both story and storyteller
When asked
Where else can one find
Justice?

The woodcutter knocks on the ground and an onion
     shakes
The story is never universal
Though it may repeat
And even symbolize, like rocks for good or parts for
     wobble
And music
With what does a story begin?
The marvellous is a cold vehicle for ink and paper
But here's an ambitious undertaking:
An attempt to account for the Twentieth Century!
Goya's small unfinished sketch of "Time, Truth, and
     History"
Was painted two centuries ago at a comparable time,
(1797)
To show Time with its hourglass bringing naked Truth
     into the light
While History writes
An Introduction

HISTORY INTRODUCES TRUTH

History introduces Truth the way Sartre introduces Genet —
as THE MELODIOUS CHILD DEAD IN ME. *It is not unusual
for the memory to condense into a single mythical moment the
contingencies and perpetual rebeginnings of an individual's experience
of history. What matters is that Truth lives and continues to relive a
period of life as if it had lasted only an instant. But to say "instant" is
to say **fatal instant**. The instant is the reciprocal and contradictory
envelopment of the before by the after. One is still what one is going to
cease to be and already what one is going to become. One lives one's
death, one dies one's life. One feels oneself to be one's own self and
another. This original crisis is the eternal moment of metamorphosis.*
Thus Truth moves outside History, into parentheses.

Person (*to the Crow*): Do you think I should head
     straight for that tree?
Crow: I'd rather describe what I would *like* your aim

to be

Person: That's an evasive answer

Crow: I would like you to make a wooden saint

Person: Does a bird need a servant?

Crow: (*The crow is silent. As Sartre says, poetry is wilful, even to the extent of keeping its 'will-to-be-unloved' a secret. This crafty refusal of reciprocity is a way of keeping others at a distance. Thus, as soon as humiliation appears, it is effaced.*)

Person: My crow isn't croaking

I must ask if he is going

He is at home to none of us

How does he know that this was all that was good

I am trying to think of his name

I should help if he has need of me

Her growing fascination with language is obvious

But what the words might achieve can be undone by
        the uncanny

Guide (*perhaps Virgil from Dante's* **Inferno** *or the
        crow from Aristophanes'* **The Birds**): Could you
        find your own country again from here?

Utopian: O no, o no!

(*The way is clogged with ivy. The vines are enormous, inches thick; he tears at them and slices them into foot-long sections with his machete; he throws the sections into a trench. I think to tell him they will simply regenerate, that he is replanting instead of destroying the ivy, but I don't; instead I tell him that I'd like to talk to him at some point, "though certainly not now," about the past. I want to know why he thinks "the scene" is dead; I say that I want him to tell me not just about his disappointment (the way certain events and individuals have proved disappointing), but what he thinks we did wrong along the way; what we did to set up those disappointments. "Will do," he says*)

Utopian: Will do!

A utopian is never surprised when someone flatters
        him with questions

In Utopia authority is found (invented) on an island

A strange phrase can thus easily debunk it

A STRANGE PHRASE

The more as foreigners we speak of foreign places, the more we dog our story, as if to give it credibility (and ourselves the virtue of fidelity). But that we've done since we began — until now, when we see ourselves (self-regard being the last resort of self-estrangement) accompanying what we like to call the last narrative, that of incredibility. But that is one which, paradoxically, records our credulity — our very lack of foreignness. So we're left thinking we're clever only because we can feel pleasure (as if that were virtuous, a form of fidelity to our commitment to consciousness, which the sensation of pleasure simultaneously threatens and heightens and thus brings emphatically to our attention) and in pleasure unloose our identity. That is, in pleasure (always suspended like meaning over words) we find ourselves as simultaneously not-yet-discovered and almost forgotten — by ourselves, the returning foreigners.

from: My Life (The Nineties)

I've never seen much   What! is the fiftieth year of my life now
that was typical   complete? such a living life? such an
    inconstant one? Imagine the film equivalent
of this, one shot per sentence, this one of.... My head is against the
scalding yellow wall, my toes have torn my socks. I keep a light in
case of tremor. I use a boarding pass to mark my place, a boarding
pass from Leningrad. As for we who love to be astonished, there's
stress on the strangeness of the past. It both was and was not I who
sat on the bed called America awaiting the television crew and
preparing a monologue on science and the feminist of the West.
Meanwhile self-sufficient wild animals in great numbers (elk,
eagles, bears, wolves, mosquitoes, midges, butterflies, deer,
woodpeckers, etc.) live spread out to the north, each allocated to
an environment appropriate to its needs, and each, adapting its
belief to the evidence, sure that where it lives is "right." Is this then
a domestic enterprise as Barrett sees it. Larry's life, Paull's life,
Anna's life. I drove to an enormous Sears, its aisles trellised,
latticed, grooved, and I walked around awkwardly with a pickaxe
in my cart, looking for a small iron skillet, a bathmat and
matching towels, maneuvering efficiently but with no sense of
being seen or of being there, capacitated, in other words,
anonymously. Short lines (of poetry) speed. Perhaps the immortal
soul survives, but let's say without any of its experience and
circumstances, released, or detached, free of death and stripped of
life—then, yes, autobiography is required. The *Tractatus's*
apparent terminus ("What one can't speak of one must pass over
in silence") seemed as I considered it transitional, leading not to
the silence of some unutterable stability but to another *extremis*, a
realm of pure alterity, for which we have no words but which we
have nonetheless the capacity to desire. Poe continues: "What we
term a long poem is, in fact, merely a succession of brief ones."
The Atlantic expands (America departing from Europe) the same
distance each year that our fingernails grow. Drifting science, the
weather sounds. She is 5, she is 25, she is 50—not anatomy. The
breasts themselves are a hunger to please. But here I can write it.

So upright, twilit, quoted, Lenin was a person. To this hand an
animal puzzles, while they, cynical, nippling war, not animal, are
sentimental. Free to give or free to receive. The American press
conceded. We were supposed to hate the war but love the warriors
and our ethics were seized in haste. Then my sister gave herself a
middle name, a word versing the world—in fact she gave it to us
all. The familial reduced to a cookbook; the family gathered for
dinner. This is a poetry of what *is* happening, nowhere
disintegrating such decisions. And I went (for the last time) to the
Soviet Union. It's hard to turn away from moving water whose
beauty is only seen in its proceeding. Across parallels the homeless
move, only singly or in pairs, since they've yet to move in crowds.
Across irritable, anxious, education cuts. A little boy playing on
the street as we walked by suddenly ran at us and kicked the man
who was with me, so we felt humiliated. The coaches shot him up
with painkillers and cortisone to cover the problem of the bone
spur in his foot and then they kicked him out of school at the end
of the season and rescinded his athletic scholarship. What had
been Model School reverted to John Muir, what had been
Leningrad was St Petersburg again. Preliminaries consist of such
eternities. One cannot be afraid to watch too long to render the
world uncanny. It seems to me that those three religions can mean
nothing more than shed of blood. It is clear that such a person as a
writer, then, not only may but absolutely must appear in our
society. On Filbert Street, on Hillcrest Road, on Russell Street, on
rue de Bruxelles, on Treat Street, on Broadway, on Mechnikova,
on Shimmins Ridge. The gestural, ritual, repetitive nature of every
meal was comforting, though it might have been coercive as well,
given our compelling memories—of tacos, mango juice, baked
potatoes "buttered" with mayonnaise, and Caffeine Free Diet
Coke (or CFDC). For any moralist the present is more important
than the past. I pause knowing that no one knows there I am. Self-
improvement is not the same as personal efficiency, and altruism is
not the same as agency. My husband was currently using a red soft
toothbrush and my wife always shaved her legs. I said that I knew
a man who, recognizing that his wife was undertaking far more of
the housework, the shopping, the cooking, and the care of their
child than he, calculated the discrepancy in hours and offered her

an appropriate monthly salary. A groggy and possibly injured or only drunk man was sprawled just behind the driver of the bus in one of the seats that face the aisle wearing filthy pants that he was now wetting, the urine dripping to the floor, and I was embarrassed as if somehow implicated though only a witness in something criminal, wrong, but unavoidable—normal—just as years before, when I was in first grade, after my friend Loretta wet her pants in class and then remained as if caught in her own puddle, I hadn't wanted to go back to school, feeling that I had witnessed something there that I hadn't been meant to see and had thus prematurely acquired forbidden knowledge. But in every situation one anxiously anticipates the possibility that a political correction must be made. The place names in the 38th line of the poem hardly signify. The lack of plot and love of detail should organize my life not according to years or hours but according to spots and stops. But to remain passive is to risk ethical mediocrity. Such a woman grabs her culture's definitions of femininity and rives them to extremes.

from: Oxota: A Short Russian Novel

Chapter 192

But to return to the theme of the novel and poetry
That is, one theme
The time comes when each individual poem reveals not
only its own internal connections but also spreads them out
externally, anticipating the integrity each poem requires in
order to explain obscure points, arbitrary elements, etc.,
which, if they were kept within the limits of the given text,
would seem otherwise to be mere examples of the freedom
of expression
One can't be initimidated by the threat of
      subordination
Nor by petty attractions nor semantic conflicts
By poplar fluff and Chinese islands
And not even by compositional imperatives
      demanding new texts
But there are days—let's not forget real days—
      when language loses speed
Then it lags as the nights lag, brief and
      nonetheless long
And one submits to a sensation
It's something entirely meaningless and unexpected
It's devoid of interpretation, a perfect quiddity
The long awaited meeting of signifier and
      signified
And one begins to examine the construction of small
resonating forms (this occurs most often in spring), to
investigate their behavior, and to extract from that a set of
—I couldn't say images—principles which seem to be the
only ones adequate to the attempt *to say nothing*

Maggie O'Sullivan

narcotic properties

PLACE A SMALL PALE-CREAM BOWL (TO SIGNIFY
abundance)
on the table-top in front of you.

Wash THE FOLLOWING LEAD ANIMALS: trout, dog,
tiger, owl, moth, wolf, cat, drake, bat, fish,
pig, dolphin, buffalo, bee, scorpion, snake,
eagle, crab, goat, salmon, turtle. IT IS IMPORTANT
TO WASH THESE LEAD ANIMALS WITH songerings-a-rung,
a-chant, a-roughy
unsway
& stirs

middles-a, haunts-a, tops-a, folds-a,
lusc
diluvian
loud lusces — that cargo, lightning: theftages.

Dry each lead animal in turn with a portable hair-
dryer. AS THE ANIMALS ARE DRY, PLACE THEM, ONE BY
ONE, ONTO A LARGE SQUARE OF WHITE CLOTH. THE CLOTH
IS GRAINED WITH A RAINONY DIVIDE. IT HAS
A RED-BLOODIED STAIN SEEPING OUT FROM ITS CENTRE.

                    HOWEVER, DO NOT
CORRECT THE OUTWARD URGE OF THE STAIN AND DO NOT
HASTEN THE DRYING OF THE ANIMALS. ENSURE THAT ALL OF
THEM ARE PLACED COMFORTABLY ON THE EXPANSE OF WHITE
CLOTH, AWAY FROM THE BLOODIED ENLARGING CENTRE.

THERE MUST BE NO OVER-CROWDING.

PLACE A LIGHTED MATCH TO THE BLOODIED STAIN ON THE CENTRE

OF THE WHITE CLOTH. WATCH AS THE STAIN IGNITES AND
SPREADS EVER MORE OUTWARD TO THE EDGES OF THE WHITE CLOTH.
WATCH AS THE CLOTH CRUMPLES, FALLS IN TOWARDS ITS CRIMSON
CENTRE.

Then THROW TALK OVER THE LEAD ANIMALS. BIND ALL OF
THEIR ONES TO UNMOVE WITH A PENDULOUS KEEP THAT
counts wing underfoot ON THE WHITE SQUARE OF CLOTH.
taint each word of that keep with a brimstone trull
(oval, fatal, henged). on the final word of the keep,
place various pieces of air, spurious to stone, so that
the last words move w/fur & pipistrelle & circles
brood to skin-broken, pinched eye.

LISTEN AS THE SKEWERED TRAMPLING OF THE DOOMED
ANIMALS ear into nethery Singes, Neighed-at's,
all knuckle-noised,
were-louds, mouth,
mouth & proves
                    Unfixed
Song-Song Stare
stood-like
fist-on-breath
finger-on-brain
madder bled meat.   maddled,

massive   amuletic   *thus-brim*   the letter of

WHAMS.   Liver

winderby   Gorple   hundridder
hind   ana   hid   hindered   huldre   hids

walkenon

AB-SUN

SOLSTITIAL, STRUCK-NINE
(whatll   wattle   'wambs
wha
white
whe
who)

leadings out
animals gone

CRUSH.
ZANZA-ZINC
BEING-ARROWED,
NORTHERLY SHEDS, SILVERY THE BYRE OF PEW
BY THE DRUM,   LULLA   LAND BY THE LOG/LANDS VOODOO
OPAL TOO DO   (FIST-PHRASES)

                SUNKS.   crown-i-slowed, Abdi

lowed, it is

RED

BEES
APART
owl-sha
conks   clays-under   splashing. Abundance. weeps.

Hill Figures

nailed Eagles   beryl   alter vasish
          Owls, Blood-bed
          Bird-gear   turbulent
          Ruled
          it,

          Raven

               blue acquiescing tar
                              thread
          the.air.it.will.be.tinned.
                         pull —
               feather against call —

Crow-Shade
plumb, true

          hemispheres
          (dwell-juggling)

               has shells,
               fan
               to
               resist —

          Skull —
               alarge, Oth

                         Twisted
                         merry-go
                         superates,
                         congregates,
                         rolled-a-run
                              lettering

Autistic   low
          twindom

to live in the Sky
to live Underground

Eagerly
as little names of both, cow, horned to begin
horn as quill
    horn thru the

            skinning torso
            tinning lengths

            fin-

            bred-

                Brinks

            Bladder-on-Stick

            hand-in, hand-outa, hand,

            sacri
            DOSAGES
            invert
            reversionary
            morrow.
             BIRTH-

                herding

            — stomach footnight —
            BIG STOOD SKULL SONGS —
            Bull-Roarer, penalty —

elved X, chema —
            tensions
            chema-
            nexions: poisons

            pins, xins,
                flicted

            rid out of hell
                reflectorised
                    — clanked —

            fanged, crowey, clotted into: buckled poly-scream
            drip wounds

            Bade.

Garb

THE TRAP IS
BENTED:
BAREWISE
DEARED

        politically emphatically in parliament today
        melted lowlands
        major misses tabloid ballast
        Breeze Mount & Delph House leukemia clusters
        flimsies in from cheek lino channels
        inimical factors
        anorexia pressed Topt Tusser
        chime warnings beams lifted

BLOOD & FAND:
FELL NOISE
AT:

        Corruptly Sized
        Gallopers Chidden
        Knock-at-a-Tooth
        Pistols, Rifles, Secondhand Riddles
        The Sleeve Alloys Only Flies
        Collusion Among Wanted
        Astringent Nouns
        Hang Air
        A Charm of Spider
        Stolen Full
        Dandelion
        Respike

RINGED BALDER VISIBLES
BODHRAN BONES
IDIOT SCRAP

        headless legless peepshow bleating
        swigment libra loada tombla

PALEO BEVELS
BICKER PYRRHIC
BIG IT FEET
& DID:

        Hag Ma Lung Ma Hag Ma Lung Ma
        Extra Fugitive Diction
        Bossed
        Plasticiser Tattooing Thus-Spheres

Crow Clattering Strictly
Ill-
Treat
Carrion Terminal
Hinges Gobbed & Wail

VERMILION
BRONZES;
(EAR MY STUTTER
EAR MY

Lights-Er Bags-Er
Flayed
Grinnel Crash the Fibres B & C Goose
Conjurations Owlyering Owlyering

THORN BULLIONS
ROCKING
TRAPS & SNARE:

Stereo Delve
Gut   Ox Sea A   Arrow Sea
Delved
Lapped Torso

HORO GEARING —
GAINERS
FLAPPIT, LITH —
URNS   TURNS
THE WIND ONCE FOR PEWTER
PEWTER
MOANS A FAIL FAIL
FUNNING BEAK:

hunger, third or shade all the dear
the hers the him-ship, what shilling dear
time was ship said

MATH-TONNER
NUMB-DIMENSIONAL

3 2 grand triple alone
thirstly these
hempen signatorial strings
Sky Rolled Over Braille

WREN HERDING:
SNAKE WANTS:

Navigational   Tin Grug   Hanged Man's
Treated Buckled Tetanus   Rock Sirens
Make

A Lesson from the Cockerel

POPPY THANE. PENDLE DUST. BOLDO SACHET GAUDLES
GIVE GINGER. GIVE INK. SMUDGE JEEDELA LEAVINGS,
TWITCH **JULCE**. WORSEN. WRIST DRIP. SKINDA. JANDLE.

UDDER DIADEMS INTERLUCE.
ICYCLE OPALINE RONDA.
CRIMINAL   CRAB RATTLES ON THE LUTE.
CONSTITUENTS   BLINDINGLY RAZOR-GUT.
SHOOKER — GREENEY CRIMSON
NEAPTIDE COMMON PEAKS IN THE
SWIFT PULLERY. TWAIL,
HOYA METHODS: SAXA ANGLAISE

SKEWERED **SKULL** INULA.

2nd Lesson from the Cockerel

RIVERCRAFT. CAREY NEON. DOVE-WEBBING FATIGUES.
THE SASHED, SILENT ONE WHO HEARS. THEN AS ONE WHO.
CONJURING SPAT LIGHTS ON THE PALATE. MUSEY TIGHT
SADDED, HAWDY KERDY'S, RAGE RUGGING JET. PORTAGE

THICKENS (NERVINE SPARROWS IN
THE MOUTH BLISTER). RED STROUDERS
RIGHT-HAND   DEW-BUCKLING WINTER, TONGUE-A-SAD-
PASSAGEWORK   OF-ALL-BIRDS WHEN THE WAVES COME
BONED, BLEED LICKS THE SWIRE-HEAD.
THE DONE-SKIRT. THE SCALDING.
THE SHOT-OVER BELLIES READ WITH
JASPER, MINCE, THE MASSIVE SHIVERS,
LOOF, SWOLE: JUTTING MULTIPLICATION.

Melanie Neilson

from: Civil Noir

As matter: of particles I may as well come down
without another word (the dream a cinema deprived
of public, cordial mitral valved lying and being
you-ed atonement, she's too sliced for landing
to rare flowered bookie arms to can't talk now
her hands are dropping big lug spora to it was more
than Friday to o' the people with a black ball of fire
inside and outside a head maintaining the rhythm rhythm
of trade trade official culture soak to simultaneously
projected toughness and warmth, cynicism and sensitivity
and as for using eyes the incidental winking and blinking
animal watch me read seeing this the tone will glint
raunchy magnificence) but first please attention please
bring the demo room up to the front desk back up to this
fresh early place

DEAR TEACHING USING EYES:
GOOD TO SAY IF YOU CAN GET IT BUT NEVER PINT AT
WATERMILLIONS WHEN JOBS VANISH WHEN BLINDS JACK
SHUFFLING SLIDING OR TAPPED IN UNCONSCIOUS
IMITATION THEM CHORDS GRABBED JUST LIKE THAT
this nod to bougainvillea lit slantindicular playing
fork in the road backed up years to this day: airish.

MEANT AWHILE THE SAME SMALL TIME:
institutional augurates
power strapped little towness intestimony to thought
(towels for instance) prosaic with psychic gore,
patriotic fizz ed distress bed; re-input Ozzy Osbourne
about a million in the afternoon...

bye-bye love cocoa phenomenal
mighty recreation privilege
mightymightymighty calamity halo
mightymightymightymighty baroque love

(at the feet of teen preacho on the hillside
miraculous military pictograph coincidentally
scorned cells, portraits of the criminally familiar
in a naturalist frenzy of expectant sails,
clouds, foam, land, cold spit on raft
the flesh swept theme of disaster
one saliva bubble of spatial hysteria tinguished...
let me tell you about this place:

Text-ray emission: graveyard weather scene
from old fruit jar information and how
they keep secret house from so & so

                                                Out to Here
...by the day...by the week...if this is a house...
the land it is on in a fency country sends no & no
letter but ploos of bare bones furniture lingual
creek counting "C-r-e-a-t-i-o-n!" thought I
better to tell a stranger (my peers, however,
are you made of?) CLIME UPSET TALL TELLING
read with difficulty the bored page is rage
spread thin as before and after *there*
the fustest with the mostest chattel indebted
plant mind hazard inauguration here ye's.

Let it be misunderstood:

    not comfort
    but coloratura
    fuzz box needer

    not safety first
    but souped up
    innards in clover

    not pursed prayer
    carpet modesty
    toy interpretation
    white cavity
    uttering space
    only

    Jot sir heavy
    moonraked boxer
    hope of southern
    california

    Stand, bow, kneel
    noetic serenade

    Moslem basketball
    league knowallogy

    Convert suite
    on totem acquittal

    not bough break
    but bit
    criminently
    lip smacked.

Room filling chemistry
devoir civique

Ultra-ultra *this* in public
tongue bath

Black sopa de dialogue
cat slanger

Hardship draft
gong in one

Abstemious facial blade
sky pierced

Self of steam
purple brain

Bevelled idiom
wig cemetery

Fractures read
dead lettre

Lush Life

Replace the world
[I want to get on]
Against the ruin
Ahoy background poetry
In some small
Wordy furniture,
Fashioning out
The specific rim
Scribbleishousness.
I shot I shot I shot
Printed the page
It goes in one eye
Thoughtness diving
And out the tether.

Twelve o'clock tails
Crow-sordid sizzles
Crow-sorted
Crossword izzles
From craw sort lulls
Crow delinquents lock necks
Crazy — O Pioneers!
Paradise of exiles
Taken away, taken back
Remember a gift to begin with
So gone
So exodus.

So many guns
So few brains
Money is nice
It don't make the world go round
So little time

Now life is quite
The hacienda
Que sorta, que sera.

Sweeten the track
Nice piano around your neck
Gets me around
And around, noose lips
A week in this dinky town
Leaves the sound bite outside
Biting sounds
Sizing outside my brain
Romance is mush
(Stop treating me like a mushroom!)
Stifling toes who moo
Marvelous ooze of oil
Dose of straight talk.

Homely adults only
With a wave to the future
Woman in the audience:
"Then why have you gone on national TV?"
[Eerie silence, cut to commercial]
Night!
Canned crying, thunderstorms, special effects.
EBB TIDE
THREE NOTE
PERFUME SET
SPACE BOUND
Writing in the dark
The windmills of your buttonhole
Unraveling three weeks now mind.
Paying admission is
Tantamount to a screen test
Something something elvis skyline.

The Sensuous Strings of Melanie Neilson
Cosmonaut or Cinderfella
A poem of
Medical suspense
Paper cut cut cut
A sense of ownership is like
A sense of lunch
"Buy"
I think we're unknown now
From here to financially,
Spiritually, telephone,
Radio, military.

To name his child
The father of Muzak
General George Squier
Played word games with Kodak and music.

Let Nature ping
Touch Nature's pings
Nervy bird coverage
Gulp the worm gulp:
Visionary position
This jacket cover's
In love
Eager young woman's head
Being held
By an out-of-frame male
Accidental hit
Heavily cosmeticized sea
So calm
So No-ville.

Denise Riley

Slip

Wodge of flat water, pale wooden sea, planed aqua block that I'm sat
                              opposite, plumped down on sand.
One reassuring flicker — am glad I am this small, not set to last that
                              long — this shivery
heat flips round my neck, coils down my shoulderblades, announcing
                              it's alright;
there are fine things in the world, then anyway it's not as if I'd a life-
                              sentence to stop in it.
So I heave up, swat off some gripping sand.

But joy at the straightforwardness of death can't see me even as far as
                              the beach café.

It was a trick of the light which made the sky go flat, the sea go plain
stand somehow erect against the sky, like a public building, as concrete
                              as the Rex
whose cinema curtains get top-lit to fairground skeletons' orange ribs,
                              stacked meaty, lined with radiant puce below
while we're hung in the dark for the programme to start, like that pre-
                              anaesthetic spell
when you hand yourself with pointless grace to a man in white with a
                              chemical smell
or those minutes of atheists' prayers, when the plane may or may not
                              safely rise
and we on board are no longer our own bodies, however nonchalantly
                              we seem to read.

I am not my body, as much as I always am: could have stayed on that
                              sand, gone coldly
calm in the stare of the sea, and an opal incision of light where water
                              slid under sky
but could not hold still long enough into that speechlessness, was too
                              loud to stay put in such death.

84

The fidget must describe
where she can never coincide.
So you'll dream you've come late to the examination rooms again
humiliated, fountain-pen lost, breathless with scouring long brown
and cream corridors for hours, though you set out elaborately early —
realising outside the right room that behind its locked doors others
in there are able to scratch away properly, to marry — then distractedly
quitting the building, you realise that a long work to determine your
own work yawns on before you, though it may find no conclusion.
Old classmates will press inward, dreamer, shrouding their lips in steam.

Then little webs hang in the grass, a hawk idea slips over the field.
I can't get to things there, I'm here, thrashing around a meadow of my
                                                                    own
that days won't end, that they will. Haul yourself hand over hand, along
the months' strings. Haul yourself in like the washing. Call it 'bruised
                                                                    milk'
then call that, Hide-your-face. Call this, No-name; who's always round
set rocking like a pot when it's time to what I may not say for the last
                                                                    bell
to shrill that I spill out onto the dusk, the frightener air, Oh Here's my
                                                                    hand

Lure, 1963

Navy near-black cut in with lemon, fruity bright lime green.
I roam around around around around acidic yellows, globe
oranges burning, slashed cream, huge scarlet flowing
anemones, barbaric pink singing, radiant weeping When
will I be loved? Flood, drag to papery long brushes
of deep violet, that's where it is, indigo, oh no, it's in
his kiss. Lime brilliance. Obsessive song. Ink tongues.
Black cascades trail and spatter darkly orange pools
toward washed lakes, whose welling rose and milk
beribboned pillars melt and sag, I'm just a crimson
kid that you won't date. Pear glow boys. Clean red.
Fluent grey green, pine, broad stinging blue rough
strips to make this floating space a burning place of
whitest shores, a wave out on the ocean could never
move that way, flower, swell, don't ever make her blue.
Oh yes I'm the great pretender. Red lays a stripe of darkest
green on dark. My need is such I pretend too much, I'm
wearing. And you're not listening to a word I say.

So is it ?

Opening mouth up to sifting rain, blurred to an o,
crouched to the green wash, swooping water,
stone arches slit to wind-cropped turf, in a grip
turn as sea-slicing gannets cut shock fans of
white water. Held shudder, sluiced in low cloud.
Where is a steady place where work gets fairly done.
Straight speech can drop out from behind the teeth
or the hands shake out clean strokes from bunched
knots onto energetic white, or long soft ropes of
line loop from the mouth, uncoil to columns
hollowed to poured sheen purity, only in shelter.
Some. I walk into a light hot wood. Inside it all
exhales, a sulky wind gets up, slings a sad mass
at the back of eyes lowered for chattering dusk,
fingers dried ochres in rough air brushed rustling
to cream hoops, strokes powdery blues tacked on
to black wire. Die deeper into life at every second.
And no self-coating slips onto my papers to make
them pulse to rooms emptied of me, they'll bear no
faint film for my children to wipe off later, so solidly
do objects stay themselves – the handwriting of the
freshly dead just doesn't get any loopier or more
archaic, as waxed comb honey would seep through
knuckles or pine ooze stiffen, domed to wasps.
Things packed with what they are. Not slatted I.
Preserve a self, for what? for ice through the ribs,
pale splinters driven straight to the heart's meat.
Calf of my senses. I'd thought out ways to grasp –
have walked straight off their edges. To dreams
of silent towns, nights, doorways, gazes, radios
on, while here a man turns and turns towards his
window, staring out over the street at dusk as rain-
hemmed curtains sway, their blackening yellowed
net. All seek a piercing charm to throb gingerly
nursed in our hands like a bird. Dear heart don't be

so strange to me but be nature. Or give me a sudden
bluish look. If I can get this far. An oil spill on the
wet road swims outwards, pleats, and flashes lilac or
rusting orange at its rim where it will dry and darken.
I think that's it. As I must think it is like this for you –
it is, isn't it. Don't tell me that edge that I never believe.

Oleanna

I'd thought you'd get through any disagreement just by talking
by persisting quietly. Fool. Steel-rimmed the hole at the centre
through which all hopes of contact plummet down in flames
as modes of talk criss-cross from opposite directions like jets in flight
which rightly never slow or swerve to read the fleecy trails of others
then something searing wipes its arc across my sight again
as rape fields of acrylic flowers do stripe your eyeballs yellow
and unreflecting green takes charge at the horizon threatening to rain —
shove off or I soak you sunshine – suppose you stopped describing
something, would stopping free you from it, almost as if it hadn't
happened?
So is that shiver down the back of the neck water, or is it memory
calling water
or is it squaring up to getting properly shredded, which does cut clean
away
from iron edges soaking into rust, from blurring fiery wells of tin-work –
someone calling tell them I'm not home, hurt me so bad to see my baby get
away, ashen-mouthed, smoking regret – instead of all that tactile surface
junk
there is this sobbing flash, you-die immediacy: who longs for decent
and consensual talk, it is that calm and democratic front I'd work to be:
I was not born to that.

Rayon

The day is nervous buff – the shakiness, is it inside the day or me?
Perhaps the passions that we feel don't quite belong to anyone
but hang outside us in the light like hoverflies, aping wasps and
                                                                swivelling
and lashing up one storm of stripes. In tiny cones of air.
Yet you enact that feeling, as you usually *bzzzzzzzzz* get to do it,
                                                                while I,
I do this. If it takes me all night and day. Oh Carol.

Song

Some very dark blue hyacinths on the table
A confession or two before dusk
flings open the fridge with loud relief
Listen honey I

A warm disturbing wind cruises the high road

where in curtained rooms children
are being beaten then so am I again but no-one's
asking for it, I'm asking for something different now

Poem beginning with a line from Proverbs

As iron sharpens iron
I sharpen the face of my friend
so hard he sings out
in high delicate notes.

A struggle for mastery to most speak
powerful beauty would run any
attention or kindness clean out
of town in angry rags.

Ringed by darkness the heart pulsates.
And power comes in like lightning.
A lion in the room, fair and flowing
twists with unsparing eyes.

Whitely the glance runs
to it and away. But let it
talk its golden talk if we
don't understand it.

Grabbed by remote music
I'm frightening myself. Speak
steadily as is needed to
stare down beauty. That calms it.

Rae Armantrout

Crossing

1

We'll be careful.

Repression informs us
that this is not our father.

We distinguish
to penetrate.

We grow and grow,

fields of lilies,
cold funnels.

2

According to legend
Mom
sustains the universe
by yelling
"Stay there
where it's safe"
when every star
wants to run home
to her.

Now every single star
knows
she wants only
what's best
and winks steadily

to show it will obey,
and this winking
feels like the middle
of an interesting story.

This is where
our history begins.
Well, perhaps not
history, but we do
feel ourselves preceded.
(Homeostasis
means effortlessly
pursuing someone
who is just
disappearing.)

3

Now here it is
slowed down
by the introduction
of nouns.

Eastwood, Wayne
and Bogart:

faces
on a wall in Yuma
constitute
the force required
to resurrect
a sense of place.

(Hunger fits
like a bonnet
now, something
to distinguish.)

4

On the spot, our son
prefaced resorption, saying,

"You know how we're a lot alike..."

He couldn't go out
on that day, but
he could have a pickle.
Out of spite, he crawled
to the kitchen, demonstrating
the mechanics of desire.

5

The sky darkened
then. It seemed
like the wrong end
of a weak simile.
That was what shocked us.
None of our cries
had been heard,
but his was.
When something has happened
once, you might say
it's happened, "once and
for all." That's what
symbols mean
and why they're used
to cover up envy.

Police Business

The suspect
spat blood and said,
"I love you," causing us
to lose our places.
We had warned him once
that being recognizable
was still
the best way to stay hidden.

Harmless as the hose is turquoise
where it snakes
around the primroses —
those pink
satellite dishes,
scanning the columns.

Was that an incarnation there
when *say* connected
with *so*? (Was it
an angel
or a Big, Big Star?)
We're just trying to make sure
that the heart's desire
stays put.

Greeting

That wood pole's
rosy crossbar,

shouldering a complement
of knobs,

like clothespins
or Xmas lights,

to which crinkly
wires rise up
from adjacent yards.

    *

I miss *circumstance*
already —

the way a single word
could mean

necessary, relative,
provisional

and a bird flicks past
leaving

the sense that one
has waved one's hand.

Getting Warm

Tingle:
a shaft must be imagined to
connect the motes
though there is no light.

The notes.
If she's quiet
she's concentrating on the spaces
between cries, turning
times into spaces.

Is it memory or physics
that makes the bridge appear?
It looks nothing
like a real bridge.
She has to finish it
so it can explode.

She is in the dark,
sewing, stringing holes together
with invisible thread.
That's a feminine accomplishment:
a feat of memory, a managed
repletion or resplendence.

Necromance

Poppy under a young
pepper tree, she thinks.
The Siren always sings
like this. Morbid
glamor of the singular.
Emphasizing correct names
as if making amends.

Ideal
republic of the separate
dust motes
afloat in abeyance.
Here the sullen
come to see their grudge
as pose, modelling.

The flame trees tip themselves
with flame.
But in that land
men prized
virginity. She washed
dishes in a black liquid
with islands of froth —
and sang.

Couples lounge
in slim, fenced yards
beside the roar
of a freeway. Huge pine
a quarter-mile off
floats. Hard to say where
this occurs.

Third dingy
bird-of-paradise
from the right. Emphatic
precision
is revealed as
hostility. It is
just a bit further.

The mermaid's
privacy.

Catriona Strang

from: Low Fancy

Respond, sweet — charity's
dubious; my quivers
solicit the same quick, not
your own cloistered neck.
It nicks censure
cuckolds a useful query.

I go all saucy at qualms
but come ploring and you'll
leave; it's transient
if richly summed: no astute
grabs it all.

Omit a must, you'd
etch culled despair
and carp a most delicate vent;
your toothy era nets
an apt senectitude, or
resets an intender's series.

It's a perturbing luxe
our studied vex detains;
as lascivious as sugar
a tender, roused invention.

No stray veer humps
labour's proper tactic —
our vital's patched; it
macerates a carnal cure.
All bloody stops inhabit us, deter
a picked guard or, no, I'm
numb — our minute familiar's
a moribund tussle.

It's a perturbing luxe
our studied vex detains;
as lascivious as sugar
a tender, roused invention.

Said I'd tilt *any* tale
if fronds ram us and
subtle foliage — thyme's
vernant. Come, best
and game me
quite chord our fit.

In patient gaming we've grazed
a cunning murmur. It rives us
a low curse, is festive's
vent, and tussles like
temper's suss — as sure
as your ratty tempest.

And still a culprit fails to emerge. In fact, everything appertaining to my unpronounceable invariably VANISHES, as though swathed in a secret register accessible only through the utterance of some VACUOUS curse, or conjured up like a fake and distant relic, a splintered production either indifferent or actively hostile to the fawning cravings of our brutal new ethic. But solely on the basis of the machinations of this alien creed, who could mistrust so persuasive a testimony, delivered in such a plausible tongue? And yet the SWINDLE remains, venerated with an intention so vile even accidental addictions yielded. "We cannot undo it," my hooligans declare.

Late nape's lit
from this rammel-full;
I'd muck an amusing bust
thigh dicks and grab mine: so nab
my chosen, fitting career.

Come contingent; you're a pressed pair —
it's a bribe as obsequious
as no paid stare possessed
and not quite dared: a verbal wreck.
Sit, tidbit, salutes are said:
            our vast pottering
evacuates simpers, or sums
            a maximum squeem.

Or come sit in enamoured regions;
I'll appall all dear protests.
Our indignant tantrums
sever a query's meek peril
and muck back loot's calm:
            presume us oscular
we sustain a choice neck
            celebrate the night air.

Nicole Brossard

Taking it Easy on my Spine

Reference
To a mechanism full of traps

What the atmosphere in this fiction?
A few words meet the oblique / effect /
a night of anonymous passages slightly
raise the wolf the fragment up to the
forehead ————— fleeing the
deserts of the eye clear horizon sliced
to the quick — bad subject.
Others revolve
The network weaves shadows for this only
end to the show

ravenous cell
tender
pronounce lips on the vein
ridiculously
to embrace you ———— mobile

rather a series of perturbations
than strange acceptance of the circuit
fades and recurs the echo
emerges again (my tongue in her
ear   relay and machinations)

a means of suspension above
the veinous blue (if I drain her
it is because she inverts my circuits
more throbbing than anything else)

AND OF AGGRESSION
arch of terror ———— chaining
the curve to an invasion
by mutating profiles

the eye turns and grows disturbed
hallucinates form narration
from green to opaque gets into
liaison
diminishes the rosewater the novel
if meandering prolongs it
dozes off tourist incarnate
stiffens with foreignness

——————— vulnerable in treebark
would have driven me thus
the anonymous headlights on the way
through the night weeds of coincidence
to join the ultimates in ink and
fragments
white spine in the circuit of vertical
lawns

from: Igneous Woman, Integral Woman

from the clamour of voices to anger
memory keeps watch in sounds
like an urging to spread out
over fogs this expression
of tear-filled eyes that have gone through
the arduous emotion of daily life
of complicity

i thought in profile and face to face
that nothing could put an end
to this skin of origin we know
splendidly in our territories
that this battle skin
knife undertow _____ eyes
that break up and bind turn amatory
phrases that address (letters)
women whose curves scintillate

this sleep (where everything began) of alerting
the woman who dreams in the abyss and the blank
sleep of deciphering (through which heat
passes) the skins of surface
in the folds and recesses and repetitions of patiences
each patience of our bodies is unprecedented
in its rhythm invents attraction
goes through our fists like a writing
an open signal

because the open veins of biographies
at top speed in our lives (because)
beside the suffering of foolish faults
of failure
rigour of the aside
all hunger like mad love
this probable imagination

(crisis) for me linked to words
(machine for divining symbols)
to the softness of lips, of eaux-de-vie
in the angle of neurological drifts

memory sketches from leaves and veins
with water all water
a monday morning of spiral in september
between the real and what flows from it
night is passing leading me
into the chemistry of the waters the women
pass through

because cities are circuses of dream
about which we think
since .... the obliqueness of fogs
in this expression we are speaking
integral, in the fog of avalanches
my woman, so that no cliché
separates us

Wendy Mulford

from: In the Footsteps

Prologue: Angel marsh

at the dark waters darkest edge
solitaries
keep appointment

grey   tide   brawling
this   night   thee
white moon pitched
half abroad where she
        Lit

                in tenebris
walking the line between sea and marsh

                in tenebris
floating the cows like funerary urns

                in tenebris
glossing the mud as the jewelled head

                in tenebris
the sea creatures near converse

                in tenebris
stupid beings crouched
in tenebris

at the dark waters darkest edge
solitaries
keep appointment

Assisi

cast me a steady toplit mountain
fill golden city walls with towers cascading roses
circle with violets dot with lilies
buff the steep sides of houses
wide the casements palest limestone mark the pavements
rosy the light on the still air softening
below the plain divided breaking
moulds lives and making

write me a cell one chair one table
candles wine at elbow
Rita
patron of desperate causes
throw out the rest

***

spittle spattle
claws weaken
hold is silence
greater than all

to give an olive-tree the benefit
head fitted to your shoulder
leaping snake tongues dusty grass
as I am blue grey light brown blown broken
live this EasterChristtide talking
brother sister round our Francisfeet the
heads bow

rapid notes dealing circles
eternity's locked triangle coins
mother son & holy ghost you'll break
my arm abject subject
reaching out board bombing
grounds no not this one spirit dedicate & virgin steady
rocks single in near-turf

*After the Italian masters, a new dispensation, she calls
(9 verses)*

*

to come come now here
& inward
being bliss
all manner of things

*

what you see
feeds your hand
your eye follows
goodness juicy

*

colour-limned eyes
turn
calling bone to bone
lip to lip
sweet congress lapsed
on god's good grouND

*

up wimple out & blow off
Timidity Guilts Equivocations Shames

*

carving the air
into terraces

*

into our sleep
sweetly jut

*

so long-ago saints looked out
from tranced bodies
full   luminous

*

pencilled trusting
        we go
off the ledge
        filling
this single steady line

*

holding memory still on dusty air
no haloes

from: The East Anglian Sequence
Part 2 (Dunwich)

Water

is which your element into air I'd offer water
sister water
useful humble chaste. makynge. in a ring of
old cold murmuring through the night you shall not have 'ee
not long this side liken to your animal
move up daily this clay and shelly bluff red remnant of
preglacial yawns

***

Sister Poverty

they took as brides
incestuous relationship
the great vase of offerings
brother leo smashed

in the world of the wretched the exploited the
wilfully the accidentally
destroyed

the strike of the heart
in a distant body
ups the odds that there's a God
but why

***

gold hard lithe hard leaps shadowward
striking a spar across the dirty ocean
loss yes off course loveliness
tall backed skyward dropping
glowing toes point back to
hammered earth

***

as lights go dancing ride out the night
close eyes to dream to navigate
open you
enter harbour on the flood
ebb impossible

Rosmarie Waldrop

from: The Perplexing Habit of Falling

The Attraction of the Ground

In the beginning there were torrential rains, and the world dissolved in puddles, even though we were well into the nuclear age and speedier methods. Constant precipitation drenched the dry point of the present till it leaked a wash of color all the way up to the roots of our hair. I wanted to see mysteries at the bottom of the puddles, but they turned out to be reflections that made our heads swim. The way a statue's eyes bring our stock of blindness to the surface. Every thought swelled to the softness of flesh after a long bath, the lack of definition essential for happiness, just as not knowing yourself guarantees a life of long lukewarm days stretching beyond the shadow of pure reason on the sidewalk. All this was common practice. Downpour of sun. Flood of young leafiness. A slight unease caused by sheer fill of body. Running over and over like the light spilled westward across the continent, a river we couldn't cross without our moment, barely born, drowning in its own translucent metaphor.

The silence, which matted my hair like a room with the windows shut too long, filled with your breath. As if you didn't need the weight of words in your lungs to keep your body from dispersing like so many molecules over an empty field. Being a woman and without history, I wanted to explore how the grain of the world runs, hoping for backward and forward, the way sentences breathe even this side of explanation. But you claimed that words absorb all perspective and blot out the view just as certain parts of the body obscure others on the curve of desire. Or again, as the message gets lost in the long run, while we still see the messenger panting, unflagging, through the centuries. I had thought it went the other way round and was surprised as he came out of my mouth in his toga, without even a raincoat. I had to lean far out the window to follow his now unencumbered course, speeding your theory towards a horizon flat and true as a spirit level.

My legs were so interlaced with yours I began to think I could never use them on my own again. Not even if I shaved them. As if emotion had always to be a handicap. But maybe the knots were a picture of my faint unrest at having everything and not more, like wind caught in the trees with no open space to get lost, a tension toward song hanging in the air like an unfinished birdcry, or the smell of the word verbena, or apples that would not succumb to the attraction of the ground. In a neutral grammar love may be a refrain screamed through the loudspeakers, a calibration of parallels or bone structure strong enough to support verisimilitude. A FOR SALE sign in red urged us to participate in our society, while a whole flock of gulls stood in the mud by the river, ready to extend the sky with their wings. Another picture. Is it called love or nerves, you said, when everything is on the verge of happening? But I was unable to distinguish between waves and corpuscles because I had rings under my eyes, and appearances are fragile. Though we already live partly underground it must be possible to find a light that is exacting and yet allows us to be ourselves even while taking our measure.

Although you are thin you always seemed to be in front of my eyes, putting back in the body the roads my thoughts might have taken. As if forward and backward meant no more than right and left, and the earth could just as easily reverse its spin. So that we made each other the present of a stage where time would not pass, and only space would age, encompassing all 200,000 dramatic situations, but over the rest of the proceedings, the increase of entropy and unemployment. Meanwhile we juggled details of our feelings into an exaggeration which took the place of explanation, and consequences remained in the kind of repose that, like a dancer's, already holds the leap toward inside turning out.

Your arms were embracing like a climate that does not require being native. They held me responsive, but I still wondered about the other lives I might have lived, the unused cast of characters stored within me, outcasts of actuality no stranger than my previous selves. As if a word should be counted a lie for all it misses. I could imagine my body arching up toward other men in a highstrung vertigo that scored a virtual accompaniment to our real dance, deep phantom chords echoing from nowhere though with the force of long acceleration, of flying home from a lost wedding. Stakes and mistakes. Big with sky, with bracing cold, with the drone of aircraft, the measures of distance hang in the air before falling in thick drops. The child will be pale and thin. Though it had infiltrated my bones, the thought was without marrow. More a feeling that might accompany a thought, a ply of consonants, an outward motion of the eye.

I began to long for respite from attention, the freedom of inter-
ruption. The clouds of feeling inside my head, though full of soft
light, needed a breeze or the pull of gravity. More rain. As if I sud-
denly couldn't speak without first licking my lips, spelling my
name, enumerating the days of the week. Would separation act as
an astringent? Ink our characters more sharply? I tried to push the
idea aside, afraid of losing the dimensions of nakedness, but it
kept turning up underfoot, tripping me. Clearly, the journey
would mean growing older, flat tiredness, desire out of tune. Much
practice is needed for two-dimensional representation whether in
drawing or rooms, and it emaciates our undertakings in the way
that lack of sleep narrows thinking to a point without echoes, the
neck of the hour glass. You may be able to travel fast forward with-
out looking back, but I paint my lashes to slow the child in my
face and climb the winding stairs back to a logic whose gaps are
filled by mermaids.

Many questions were left in the clearing we built our shared life in. Later sheer size left no room for imagining myself standing outside it, on the edge of an empty day. I knew I didn't want to part from this whole which could be said to carry its foundation as much as resting on it, just as a family tree grows downward, its branches confounding gravitation and gravidity. I wanted to continue lying alongside you, two parallel, comparable lengths of feeling, and let the stresses of the structure push our sleep to momentum and fullness. Still, a fallow evening stretches into unknown elsewheres, seductive with possibility, doors open onto a chaos of culs-de-sac, of could-be, of galloping off on the horse in the picture. And whereto? A crowning mirage or a question like What is love? And where? Does it enter with a squeeze, or without, bringing, like interpretation, its own space from some other dimension? Or is it like a dream corridor forever extending its concept toward extreme emptiness, like that of atoms?

Deanna Ferguson

Sisters of the Even Jesus

Heels unmoved in pure opposition drive the snub at various tracks.
Versions equate between patrons and liberty as an omlette of man.

Do what? Wall darkens as the second is lit, bulgy-eyed in an
eagerness to know. Completely foul to be emancipated, by the
vital beauty park of principle.

I should like some coffee, some personification
            of demon as genius
            some symbol of symbols
            some feign of salvation

Wrought on spit and reason system for knowing shingle or brick
noises flesh-out-flesh.
                    Carpenter cones ivory lift center rest
                    entering lifted round chordal snaps re-entered

So brains shall go in slippies, weeping, washed, clear-sighted.
                    He stands for John
                    and she stands for Mother.
                    So John and mother are antecedents.
                    She looked at John's brother
                    who had rushed to defile her.
                    Whom did you send with him?

Brat habituated likewise nominated alive but snuffed at a luminaries
outing. By reason of flanks the junk held. Not at all tot shredded.

Purified dragging to decamp totality. However the zephyr indisposed.
Consequently her suffix as if leaked or needed.

> The person could warble on
> and on. Sustain it elsewhere.

Citizen by what methods still do particles fade? Miles lease change
not original I. My occupation (not do not wot?) conduit—is what
reaches chief.

Revolution of loft from lack in this place. Establish overheard for
it is so exheedingly troublesome recounting.

No smirking. Rank side route out honour. Crack dissimilar obscure.
Exterior by the empire. Peculiar to my caste. Go about above go
fair.

It's Bad For You

Had I seen square when
eyeball suture teethed with
cankorous proclivity I
could of died to prod behind
my high-heeled professional the
way spat hangs off
edge of a chin. Zuzu petals
herself as pucker in putative
puts off yet imported pastrami
sends. Build to bang, bend.
Soaking redresses life's
expectancy, puffing
a major cause of smart disease. Picks
include co-ed doggy push-face, call me live
at home. Soap Ken's moan. Down
Antigone's hospice, earthward
a shift outright. Alone, a looney, what birds
of killing worth raddled in the twilight sequel.
Age as ass rode the knight divina cleat Oh
stupid Love, ain't I astonished.
Crude cleave garbled that cadenza
look it up. Goon gone as deed. Double
digit bum-out. Like so much cake
and *having* to eat it, the girls
are hungry the ladies
weak the dames
dead and same please
should beasts be freer than we? Please
I'm a thinking thing, a public stew
(pussy melt hearts thru the kidneys)
a tall blonde dumbell with a vegetarian nugget
(Goodness Goddess Idleness)
elles like chicken le cheap like fish. I've
had it to my neck, imaginary bowel, soured
tummy, hit the lights

hampers chompers coast
wreck cut this deck various
logics capture thee. Drunk
having sex with mom
in the lavatory. Assume to say
and lack good company of confession
paralytic revelation parasitic
empty ephiphinied the rhime. Fear
of fine, nor better to booze up and riot
than diet against ache of ennui and hang
of wasted time. Nor
better to smell out of fear
than smell fearfully. Law and
odour for coop and keeper. This my blood
given to you. Take it, and know
that you owe me. Next stop
rest thought
under the musky musky sky
by a scintilating sea I went to see
and saw it, and something else
forgot it. Squeeze the moment, train
the package, equipe the underknit that
dreams drive. Hertz arrives as
just my way of getting on line
from the dip of my chip, ticklish at
the t, to touch littoral lamp post.
Dim city squirt, how was drifting then, when?
Crane hi low bed other. We take our mind off
your load. Straight Express, sta*r* right
defunct, like so many bell bottoms
caught in the chain, gallery white
original loci is it really like this? who's
my little whatsit? Ask about method now
and I imagine I hear the vacuum I see
"the sense comes back, not I"
But. Baloney
don't have holes
you mean

mock loaf
with its bits of bones
but no, those are
plugs not holes. So badged
myself Complete & Me
gnostic suction revealed thyself and if
the glue seeps smear it. Much like this
springs must have a shag, a better Will
the slick slope built
a hot-house pulse. I mean
go kindly as I think lest the
'pholstery kibosh
rings 'round the sink. So much
shot over powder, expansionism a louder
atopic. Got you under my skin
(over the ocean) Swim! and get the landscape
right and the characters will follow
getta a braless gimmick if ya get agenda
glib lib common from ungrateful dust.
Extruflux. My timer
has only one tempo. Top to
bond rapid wrong response.

ad ream

(after A.S.'s)

Fear why it's dame sin rapt in lovely leeches. Glances spike many rooms do, strays today spilling of dream. Love disdain the rig chapping from crazy, calligraphic mold in needing corruption. Who will love between need and knaw. Herein the slur to have been another's lies. In blur of the sing, hellos burn for kill innocently. Swirl the meaning oust, swing that allowing might. All stains on who make through their mind.

Bombs can stun in aplomb melt doubt conforming mine. Fate arrogance mirrors some lauded mess. From chordal dress stitch part of a mention. Immenses a mass reeling off horny throes; what kinder ploy chains a darling. Wine dwindles down to a precious brew. Neglect smirking as the action. How played would you feel? Distant systems by word, let's heal with them, not kneel to them.

Today a food meal estranges what is mental in course. Must of peeped scared and that gives us the wool upside our eyes. Does you do the voice yourself round in the crate joinery of anguish. Sentient down to its reprobate bed seems good enough for me. But how, razing curs of force, can loss articulate more world? Homage without evolved rancor like hot wheels, the most churned reason is lodged. I growl on, stung instead of screaming out a coward's lament, instead of a reactor's door, or a volt ground in rhyme, or still a little nature less a tune heard.

Udderly the boonies muse are us. Sly hose slide under her seat quiet like suction made this tense ebb open. Sunday hags reverse loaded dawn, three's anoint, bereft of up market biding, cakes in the face. Burned into one skin's living scarred from other's takes. Trucks load up skids of fact determined by bills of lading. Until to slid off at mono rail, pulling on my own star.

A wetness roles in many rivulets. Dew past the feet her bodice splits, cherry lips, heady clam. Unchained at the start or mutations concealed as living up to a person. Panic, from within, or upon us? Laugh laugh laugh laugh laugh laugh laugh. Morose at the proper point and the quotient is told. Trances and seizures hired to question. She is something, a spot cognizant because others are here.

Hannah Weiner

from: silent teachers

CLAIRVOYANT STYLE
SEEN WORD OR HEARD

why we hide ourselves   put them down as you like it
we destroy interference   agitation   funny spell
by straightening hair   strong line above hints
wave   they say it might be something like that
your interference secure   read scientist   mother
vanishes   somewhat embarrassed   not up to para
be sure   read books   follow instructions   between
paragraphs   bend me westward   softly out west
different   page one   get off see simple
advertise   put them in gently   put in them goddam
miracles   since
subject illusion is illusion destroy selfish   some
personal identities   seen pictures are illusions
include holograph   where is it   some punish it
we ask questions it   answers provided   like black
children also   also drumming   heart beat safe
tender indi   put your heart to your drum and see
if its regular   unlisted provided for   cereal boxes
off the shelf   keep clear   cheer up   many black
children hungry offside eager   many more children
we graduated   great big lesson   only survivors
press tender obsolute   suggest illusion   old
hippies great   same again westwa   preserve life
cold water only   subject enclosed   ohme   spelled
correctly   add letter   dear who dont wear belt
professor buckle   somewhat attractive
bad intestinal   shock also be brave sir   add bro
sir russell   but he wont do it he wont do it
russ just bend   put practice called praxis in perfect
hann thats subject   get off it   some material also

let it go   sir sure   some however wear   hann
identify   enter graduation   complex identities
chawho   cant spell indifferent   turns into
Green monster if refused   blah   white teeth
grrr   hann next   ron barrett objects   help
me help me peter   somebody listens carefully
give me andrew levy   umph   forgodsakes the
children know more than me   enter graduation
learning beginner teacher   forgive tenderness
exact exactitude   hurry it up a lit afraid
he oh forbid Green monster humph   only instructions
appear   godzilla important   lizardee changeree
dont include name   sit james ha   secret last
book sequel   put barrett in   simple teacher
submit agriculture   communist teach   brave
send by picture offset   Why wrinkles   west coast
finished   include me   three women missing
sand   cut the stripe and flipe the ripe
elle hell   penny full of grace   umbled   draw
table   write me   send postcard even   barr
much luckier history   content   subscribe   put
in them able   oh score   pictures offset set
aside ohboy see   clean hear   plus indians dear
i forget um hero   cant drink with
power   concluded it either   some people can
some people cant   mother wouldnt include any
more instructions   aar tippin gives them all
great big forgotten leader   sir sar   get off
switch radio   ohboy religious holiday
rituals forgotten   hann they control with it
despite arrogance   always albeit bruce friend
henry hills   move still   complete above   noa
rich cancel   page offset   simple teacher
preface   ohboy me   seven century   name sir
picture who illusion   he strap outside   be
brave he children   um count keep secret
hann hard   opposite refuse contractions
osbmit   require illusion suspender   submit

sis listening   oh goddam director
sir upset has put his coffeee table on his
secure   say it in english   ohboy char
tableward   aunt hannee   fe please green
lizardee   hann thats no potatoes odd   sir
char ambulance driver get bruce in   bruce
leader   cheer on asa bob harr sklar
kill er with the people if she nar   sobeit
hann some upset has been upset   sir seemingly
director plus association   grab em   holler   thats
indecent   ohboy follow instructions   pinch pants
hann thats secure old lady   sis forgiven   plus
sente   bruce endquit   only six paragraphs lost
sir bruce sir bruce repeat sir bruce   who is writing
this goddam manuscript anyway   ron hints   survivor please
sir handicapped omitted   sis difficult situation
ohboy bruce ladder climb   falloff   beside tree
catchya   sir official resident   get screw   plus pool
holler scream   mother adds appendicitis from overeating
kindness   please omit jelly   subject   thats queer
sir silence subject get off the page   cath abolish hint
sir able to silence subject sir   ohboy
oh forgodsake put silent instructor in blah bleat sneak
admit monster   also Green   also swears
aunt hannee please very polite   hann char
forgive knows who   goddamit   when silly   push
curtains aside   disguise hide aside obey hints abide
sir secret silence is sir bruce content   submit object
sis content   forgodsake put in the dont rush goddamit
he makes me sure   forgodsake get goddamit   spelling
error off the continue   hann thats honest cure
put goddamit back in again   let him plush sofa sit
back sprain   hann hes absolutely confident   absolutely
confident and you arent out west get it   hes strong
mother likes push   handle gently   only ron knows
him   put another in   like rose   confident   spelling
get grow   push upward   falldown   short   we introduce
people   two confident   noa kle walker we   ti im gonna be

softly softly i put the book down by my page
hann please hann please write another
i feel guilty   signed andrew   han thats his subtitle
forget ignorance   projection   we are all glad together
catchem   some intelligence   quote   absolute
confidence   some kind   some relax   see me only
curl   object   hes attractive   inclusion   parscene
we love silent obedience   hann hes strict   wife
wild   hann hes stuck for his next object   true
well yer better meet jude
sitter   bless   quite comfort   somewhat wild agree
organizes   somewhat bore   mother publishes origin
old magazine news   had newspaper cranston once
end paragraph soon   some plus   hann its ended
add melan   oh poor perfect ended
melanie has to correct herself   otherwise some people
listen to it some dont thats the difference signed
strict orders   have confidence   sis repetition
anger hostile   subtitle abrosion   kick em hard
mela forgive concile jessica ind hunt   ma she
can pictures show   finish your article
passive obedience   hann dont bend   obstructure   simple
knee loose   confiscated   ohboy tremble   i cant get
home   poor bill honey we poor dear poor dear
obstruction   sir russ hide   ohbeware   underwear
wear white   communist invention   out west we hide
forget suitcase   employ agent   your making it ugly umph
oh agent come   send some peter IN see light around
                    undefeat sobleet heal
oh boy guard   simple people   carry suitcase   indifferent
believe intrusion   put russ away   forgodsake hes
over seven feet handsome   hann thats a large man
                    forgodsake yellow
suitcase   can ron silliman be carried downstairs
by goddamit   wish paragraph   ancient   hes a guidance
couns   anyone else   suggest illusion   get prayer in
old jackson   scrub   retire   old   say have you any
secure   goddamit jackson behave   older woman also

kick yourself off the page stupid and submit   oh insolent
boy   he tremble   sir barrett watch   sir scram   bad
witch   obtrusion   get em page clear   hello hannah
im wild   invention   plus purple square   dont scare
people   oh insolent agent   squares shows himself dont
russell deal   oh poor last paragraph   russ hides
emergency   confident   sir square   confident   blow
hard   sir agent occupy   sir silence   get off page
quick um   oh bold author Green   aunt hannee irs me wheee
obstinate   scrum   poor boy   insolent boy
insolent oh perfect add picture
get off some insolent   sir serious incident   forgodsake
shut himself up   clear page   ron in sir hide director
out west   um page   so lan we hide   black understanding
dinner table is what its called in the holy bible
temperature   sit around   just finish page umbrella
sir script   ron object   get in under table   ron
oh embarrass somewhat indulges   be careful now   ice
cream dish   barr suggests subside   slightly forgodsake
goddamit   embarrass   we treat people   objection
hann cant she abybody cruel can be cruel   put it down
switch   subliminal other   treat people two page
old   continue   get square   ohboy we cross our
intelligences   some transfer   some guilty
oh boy stream across   we build   oh dam   darling
perfect   youre hurting yourself dear   my habit
silence please   interrupt me   have confidence agent
some friend   pause   close personal   personal ice
cream is in my personal dish   please subject enclosed
perfect switch   absolutely no sugar drink unless
confess some hint drink able slight   some do   some cant
get excited   words hungry about cheap   interjection
jackson relaxes   forgodsake i never touch sugar sugar
unless its in sugar   no cereal goddamit   breakfast
i know excuse   plus promise   slight headstuff
ugly   ignore entire sir   little heart ron seen
trouble   encourage poor   hann poor darling you
are in it again squit   one line oh perfect satchid

has a cup   we drink careful   see most hurt   some water subside
please place yourself in your own position   chilly
day   upum flags   who guessed wrong   breakfast order
one guesses french toast   suggest indifference   say
who color   what spelling   white continue   crazy horse
safety   twenty   count again ma   fourscore
teachers amongst us   hann just simple
put she before   makes me appears on time   sis only
object waiting   who guesses   follow stretch   hann
dont cheat   peculiar sausage appears on plate   condemned
repeat who guesses   none   laugh   put them crackers
in   six silent editors cross their feet hoping you
will die before them drink coffee and see them
try crossing shes path with fire   hann thats a very
indignant man youre writing about   sir disappeared
in lan   hold on   condemned building   crossfire
stretch   let walkers   prosecutor   let him be
cant control   mother excellent prosecutor   oh indians oh
subject guess wrong   can never tell hint   her silent
we begin page again   hum   guess cards   oomph collapse
her mother cant do any psychic interference research
oh well   excellent breakfast   slightly hostile feed
good agnostic   believe strict attendance   behave
well at school   suggest old house   sir dream oh was
fire cruel door   stove lit   grandma   hann it was the
house subject next door complete   three grandmothers
sit in a chair   ohboy vision vision   grandma here
complete   sir color   goddamit her three mothers three
sit in rocking chair chair   beside bed   oh vision oh
complete oh page number oh my mother her mother all secret
complete education   safety first   per silent
per underground solution keep twice obtrusion
very silent   we win all   complete education
unlept   forgive   unrest   typical underground
out west solution twice praise keep silent
we leadership above include   sorry no list   welcome
home who next   abi   struck   her illusion   her guess
we workers   all   um silent   godzilla prayer   important

ohboy a new thing to think about   say unforbid   prayer
umph humph rumph   ohboy another   dont worry stupid
agnostic   we pray alone   clear   havent heard from
sur suggest   mother cheats   her silent her obey say
twice invent   get college selfish instruct   ohboy
another   careful mother organizes mother town
sent should be the last line   sixteen years silent
writing   ohboy mother laugh   someone else abroad
tell my insent i can handle it if known   silent away
crosscurrents across   no matter we mind   long time
ago travel   umph   barr quit barrett   we all mind
we all just a line scare   be careful   nobody knows
who humph   old ind friend ohboy cut short ind name
careful get it together quick figure it out for
yourself   old laughs   ohboy   oh bore count   600
pages   have you ever left content   publisher correct
general subversive contest   scene over omit   put
communist fellow old days   asa took the death card
made it red   plenty abroad can spread
who scrimp   allowed ind   name jumps   sir name old
traveler jumps should be overheard   either way or
you communist speaking   old indian heard
sir successful indian   sir bill   contempt of rempt   be peace
happyville   oh bill   sir A   contempt   subtempt   justhump
american A   capital letter   have you seen   sleepytime
oh judge   oh bill   han have you initial ever been
unmeanpt   sir initial   just hold unto seatbelts   whom
weather   peter INman
golden aura sits on a capital letter   how did these two
get together   um   hurgh   burgh   brumph   hrumph   do
                    we dumph
han honey be relentless be   we clean land up   sir courage and
sir bail   mother says we sit we mail   we flail   contempt   have
courage   court sir   sister kick it in we A boy   oh boy we judge
have you ever been with an A principle teacher   hurry
we have twice around   sir title   sir book   boy
are are you stingy   tough   hann laughs enter
stir into oldtown keep quiet   just let people hit

obstinate college   hann she could scare help there
where recognition   oh boy provcontrol   you skipped
us   strong healing is almost underline see book
careful *retreat* adver *claire*   sir serious   risk
advertise   perfect consideration   omit
constitution   please regards   old broken treaties
oh should be the next line   sir comfort here   old
trailor truck   some indian hut   sir heard
sir computor child   umph umph cut double
computer schedule um humph   put down pen per
child per darling   are you large enough   oh boy   oh boy
a miracle   can you speak   i am electronic
oh hum   i am wonderful fuff   oh hum
my mother is   oh boy computer style   low voice
last day christmas i was   oh boy poor dear child
has spoken hidden collect evidence oh short
we all love you dear   my seven pages last   oh dont
finish   oh boy i am wonderful   cheer child   oh boy
whatchamacallit   i transfer my intelligence system
can you read me quietly   oh boy delirious   age
underage voice   low computer speak   i have a
machine to teach   can you count on me   brother
fled   mother was   oh boy supergirl   tell super
brother please i am intelligence   oh mother poor
sir char humph   oh quit   machine   computer child
older woman now   poor dear   whatchamacallit
sir *fast*   conflict about period complete   famous
oh boyme   child doesnt know me   electronic please
sir name   hann i object to antihistamine
drowsiness   not traveling when asleep   sign
pills continue   screw it   be careful now we are a
machine part   oh boy   godforsakes a fresh mind   um
eleven   i am broken treaties promise
yes but are you eating
carrots now   promise me you will be a big boy
and return to your mothers side answer this question
please omit name   sir hum   child   funny girl
old bro   speaks   boy

i'm glad to know you too   careful
sir sister sir sister sir sister sir not mention sir name
put careful now   sir remember aside cheat like
sir name oh   um computer   finish the
article stupid   mother he cares for me   jan slump
sir tell sir truth   sir tell sir truth on sir page
forgoddamit   surprise   where child   broken treaty
sis *spoke*   book um   forget style
oh boy treaty   oh boy treaty   for lar stu
conflict   sir page return   solace goddamit plum
sorage   confleet   sir james admit   sir glad   two
piece   sir child lost   ride hum   old treaties promise
sir book hum   oh following horse   let em ride hide
subliminal education department here   oh boy   we
dream   holistic   sir advertise   sir quiet   sir
hum   official   sir char weak   careful now
oh godzilla prayer   we continue to research alcohol
never after scared with   after school   demands
hire repeat endurance   sluggish   obey district
can handle subliminal   cheat obvious   call stuck
people contract   oh boy cont cost   no phone
explanation   contest   have confidence   some
tricks pulled   great leader stand   russ sir
learn from standing   who hears   you complete
from clear   sir water wave   hold complete
subliminal voice stand   wont give an neither
nor chas monster either   please include me aunt hannee whee
reading continue   ron
hurts   umbleed   sir hold   concentrate   audience
sir   oh crowd   sir ubliminal understanding
cheat   um hold finger   unbleed   sir court case
subliminal prop   confess goddamit   see page unflete
audience   strict control   large crowds umph   ohboy
me   oh poor ron controls   unfeed   perhaps schedule
crowds together   mother says audience   big control
oh my god shes halfway through   lew
hes speaking in his sleep
ma he works best when he rests

oh poor   otherwise limit   perhaps control conflict
breakfast now   old sole   perhaps stuck   water unfit
sir audience control problem   sir crowd large
goddamit get him off the construct my dear
audience conflict   silence instruc   goddam page
honest sir i compliment book unlist   sublime
keep still   goddamit close page   ron unfit
bob dylan ol hippie great record hear
historical blast   ultra sublim   contact
be careful now   we power we teach

Carlyle Reedy

The Slave Ship

chain beat me to death 3 am the 2nd
clattering against a door tonight I
    not slept I   all *its ring links, only clank*
smoke   lost return   *on the bone of my body*
head,   temple, *all over*   *to neck*   breast
in   pagan blue, plunging, *I so naked*
intake to belly   buttocks, the charms
they put you under, *it is not good,* what is used
with chains they put you in, in the hold of the ship
    on in   the human in
    the white voices *sometime some one amongst us* sing
    change   in the mortal   save   the body
next to you would rot, hot all the time in the hold
    it does not heal,   do not hear
I want to hear, I   believe   I be
the story of   *blue black work of god*
    their voices come down through a hole
    words   fail, is it possible
    one he die and black blood rumble out his throat
put like   if this death   then
he twist up stiff going on   redemption,
    next on   *side of him she did not move for fear*
    self   deathless   *him go all stiff*
    she stare into nowhere like to live on the truth
    live without any other food but truth *after*
she never right in her head after   and *die*
many   *die* and some will not over
Port-au-Prince she thin all the time
she walk roun because the test   *hard* on
their poor bodies,   *she don't know where she be*   *If only care*
she   *not die yet for awhile.* Only an old
self *I went down*   *the hole with my sister*
    make living awhile   if it does not,

in her pile of rug she had   *I had a pile of rag*

did I smell bad, It don't smell alright   the love
all there, *god's love,*   *Love all,* not
the reason being nobody but one   mother
is all, *put a chain on her she leg   she so thin*
    small possession   doled, each sip parched
out it fall away from her   away all her skin
it tore by where the chain slap the back
all around   in us,   the same
if you could die, you would like that
peace   if you could
      you could sleep   get up off the chain
                    love   all attention
she told me because she young and pretty
those men June 2nd 8 a.m.
she without that   dark   you could see
like a rose, she bruise up for absolution
      in the route, no help, no harbour
      you hope maybe that ship put into
to be saved.   important and big
in white lace, she all time set by that captain
things which happen in this humanity, in
      landscape of the roses with   leaves

the cook pot she banged on it with the silver
thorns.
                as a guide in   terrain,
what is happening *I got to tell my story*
again the chain beat me onto the death,
    losing individuality in some greater
clattering on the iron ring   the ring
                they stood up to say we have
      caught *on the bone of the   woman*
by years of study   discovered
come here over to me but I came over
knowing this is not   being at the crux
                for that bone, you could hear

fast on the idea of   indivisible
it crunch and crack and saw the sea
over her body but then the man .... turned on to me.
i   *hoped to get out in the sea over the side*
    that moment much   unseen, being
removed, *pleading for about 3 days*
to throw myself quick over to be lightened
on   contrary   *even to forget my poor sister*
I   ready and strong   then the man in stow
he come up, with it all slow
living without for *I in awful pain, crackling*
    body temple crumbling down in an illusion
    sea so flat and black I could walk
sense disempower   soul   victim
    my leg all held   that was very great/weight heavy
                only a babe on a link *was left*
to whom *that he held back my arms so I could not* reach the babe
now in   time   soul infused   each cell
reach across there, *in very slowdown time, she dyin' I saw that baby* die.
in the value of adversity rise conditions
    lead the echo   soul back to its original
sound   like she bag of sighing dust all the breathe
came out that woman and she die right there.
divine   action   taking place
he pushed and beat on me til I back down
    I fell...   it is safe to be alive   to be love
            peaceful with   trust in the lord
    I got myself awake my sister she say I sleep
one day   one other   purity   *she*
fusing with purity of non-matter come to try
she can bittersweet fall on   the sharp plank
    cut herself in the dark, the deep earth,   the body...
I wanted to change overnight find that woke up without bein' there
feeling   some dream   affliction
    solitude *after she die in the hole*
    I cry for so long I don't know
tremblings and fears   screen-out   sorrow
                the creaking of that ship

in all my life, I have carried as a weight this
smell   death   to the healing
   can such to look neither to the left nor right
nor make any concord   *not to make no move*
to call attention   *with rats which ruination on*
the skins of   feet, defeat   one devil
as god's child,   comfort   mother
heartbroken   her story   hear

once time all told about the slave galley
in the ship's hold.

birds
tongues
nipples
jelly

limbs
plums
lobes
sheets

groaning   blackened   they push
flooding   they crush   they thrust
break   they tickle   dark

licking   slick   hot
dying   juicing   beating
drenched   hard   flesh is

quickening   flying   sweat
tingle   dipping   sweet
heaving   stung   meet

hearts
buttocks
passages
thighs

cries
strings
marble
tender

The Bedsits

CHAIRS   MANTELPIECES
TABLES   CATS
VASES   PIPES
NEWSPAPER   FACES
LINGERIE   BOOTS

SAT UPON   CLUTTERED   CRACKING
BLUE   FOR EATING   IMMOBILE
RANGED   LINING   OF PORCELAIN

SMOKING   FLUSHED   TALKED
RATTLED   SMILING   KNITTED
BURNING   STARCHY   THEY WOULD WEAR

TO READ IN   BY WIRED   MUSICAL
GRIMY   REFLECTING   DRESSED IN
INK SPATTERED   PADDING BY   SLIPPERY

RUGS
CHESSMEN   MIRRORS
PEOPLE   DISHES
GAS FIRES   TOILETS
RADIOS   ANTIMACASSARS
                                                BOOKS

The Blue House

Of the tree
The monkey
  seated posture

Those sharpened points

The parrot
  hair of
reclining posture
in the still of life
locks of her hair
white hand of

of a bone
of a Christ
luscious
unlascivious

of the Portrait

* * *

Death   above

curls of a mare
pulse
as one is
teeth of shell

Planted
  be
To be seen
Blood in a white skirt
Verity Coyoacán

in the Vine
of a Balance

of a bloodheart
always falling
float

an urn of shells
the death mask
To be heard
Swoop of folds
Scroll silent

in the Root
of a Melancholia
of lipstick
  connector
what spits out
in amphorae

  suckling
at last
To reach

* * *

Flame

Wings of
White Hiding
My blue
after Portrait
Where I light
I twisted
IT Atomic
Metropolis
saddened Moon

Blood falls
Death Head
Umbilical
the wish was
Exquisite corpse
Before those fires
IT ROBOTIC
false polish

Touch
Birth
girdle
those many
heat over
Gringolandia
IT Dominated
Pomp
Struck flame

Under Mother
harp
in a world
these poor
IT Death
Monopolies
O Bleeding

***

Indigo

Green   Snake-like   Goddess

Home of orange   Peony explosions   Pure serious

Hairs arranged

Expressionless   To be paired   To be   flow

as grow old when young to be

young while old,   mossforest green   close to breasts

in ribbon shoots   a child   plain

queen   witch

a bird   real   in a leaf

seer

daughter   of a snake where root strangles   butterflies

white

COLOUR

like a cut   like a scar

The Portrait

EVE THE FIRST of knowing all her eyes
in a river Tooth of Death sweet flesh This apple
Green To be torn of Death curing the world
By her womb upheld along a fresco MESTIZA
FRUIT HYBRID AT the EDGE A few corners cut & damaged
Sticky honey in a prayer she is that all live
squat down of the SEX WILL PUSH in a River
That the
species live very poor she says who is the first
By DISAPPEARANCE who grew fat who were these terminals

Milk in a cut in a scar in a vein
Blossom wild skin Symposium
Calves grip FEAR Supine
in a skin strangled her votaries her pantheon
Voluptuous in Pain

around her neck aloof unclothed upon A BED
in torso To sell a straightforward FIRM
IDOL STATUE PITH FACE
SEDUCTION DEDUCTION A seeing Animal

She must watch
BE TORTURE EROTIC REDEEMING
Determinant Rekindled her immanence Across all
Formulation Venal Silk White State DESIRE
SAID RAVENOUS Drips as Honeycomb interwisted &
BITTEN
For the skin
of one BUD Savour of BLOOD Thy Honey & Milk in a swollen
carnivorous Born independent ARDENT SHE LOOKS

***

Geraldine Monk

James Device Replies

I wasn't here   I was here   I won't
here I wasn't   here I was   here I
wasn't was
here
      today gone to
fora feeble
      bit part
      my tongue off on
      off was was not
   here was I was not I t-here I was here me
HEAR ME
w-here was   why was
they was draggin me
to won't here along
      to wasn't here my
      part bit
      snip-snippity
      my strut kicked feeble
tongue lollery
      lip-s-titched to-g
buggered and frog marcht t t-here
      w-here I was not
      HEARD

Anne Whittle Replies

a deal more
crafty than
uz
they knew
things never
uttered
in words
arms length and
longer than a
think
thi med id up
and coming out
with things never
born
till pushed and named
from their gobs
lying
withershins
they knotted uz proper
in tittle-tattle
&
chains
*

straight up they
crawled
between our brain-curls and
pin-winkled out
ower
tight black slugs of
monosyllables

Fox Trot

weavy path
>> magic quake
>> trot
> hot brick
>> red
> paw sore
>> blister brain
storm fit
>> shudder limbs
> seize throat
>> choke neck-a-neck
>> croak
> wise words
>> weep meat
>> possessed
> meat moved
>> I was moved
I was moved to go up
> to top (IT)
which I did (IT) was so
> very steep and
(HIGH) I was come to top
> (IT) the hill high (I)
saw sea to top it the hill
> (I) (HIGH) saw (IT)

The Football Hooligan

Yeah atz me un
ere a gow   ere a gow   ere a gow
'obberish jing
                Ow
                   God Save the Mob Wave and
                                     Jack Flaggers
ga-gaa   ga-gaa   ga-gaa
              coochy-coo
              mugger fluff
                  un
              FACK YOU

The Poet

Fack you?
                Doesn't sound right.
                Like a rude rush of loutish worrystorms
                        (cold blood-bergs)

All night
                I've been searching for
                just the right words

Maybe
                If I crawl into bed
                they will come to me.
                Naturally.

Angles

thisa one
off a
shoot at
angles
from side
to zenith to
down deep-
estRange
about t
urns cork
screw a
gain ca
tch wind
ow
frame re
flect f
lick knife
points
of
glasshine
glint re
BOUND to
RE
    gret

c
reased up
slang
matching
di
sect of
word
playing
Time by
ear

mouthing
barb-s-
piccato
spin rift
    drift
wonder
relics
from spine
up star de
lux
to
astrocyte

RUSE
ruse ab
  use
ing voltage
for fun &
game
changing
part
ners two two
timing paso
doble
automated
interrupt
of cadence over
and out
OUT now
symbiont
precision

con
volutions
spiral gyro
scope of
much
and more

behind
the breach that
thought that
nought that
note so
final
B flat B
nothing
O B Just
joy riding
out on limb an'
thanat-an-atom
      E an-
        atomical
to infin
con
   brio

DRAGON   FLY   HOWLING   MONKEY
softly   softly
lacepale
rustlings basically what
you get in skeletons this
side of hell
                fragmented
                            smoke/croak of internal roughness
                begging for movement
accommodating dance bands
so apt so
go-go so
                phobic contortions fly &
                howl agro-
                            vating bottle-
                                        neck wrapping chatter
                                        flap a
                                        flap

'El Caballo Raptor'

lunar masque

an equine head rears   a womans face bleeds white
prehensile lips   before ruin
bloodsucking and hooked in   two black trenches
rapacious horse play   crush down on cheekbones
crested and swollen   charcoal on chalk
with frenzy   choking black ivy

stricken
seaquake
of
iron limbs
overwrought
straddle
airquake
and beyond
the aftermath
unblinking
the eye of a squid
devours
their future shadows
stretched and melted wax
frozen
partners in fatigue
seething
webbed and fossilized exhaustion

Karen Mac Cormack

Multi-Mentional

That line's running-board basics
sidereal on all fours
preen
exploitation of perfect timing
renew
maximum syncopation
temperature tantrums clever yes
but mongrel
statistics are with us.

Head up in arms
pieces of time at regular intervals
if the ring fits answer the phone
non-commital background
indications assume no one's perfect
telepathy
soft patience or landslide afloat
the birds not flying pinpoint
a simile swerving away.

Resex   (the stub left on a pruned branch)

obscure freedom from orthodox
forever irritable endowed
good-natured as rustic
not two-edged hurrying to without never with
invincible slanting
unable to exit boastfully
provoking incurable
a little merciless displeasing
destroyer invisible past folly quick
insatiable snap
denial persistently
unlucky standard about virtue pledge
newly disdainful
to snort with dice-box ballot
glad-eyed yawn marked pantomime first golden
a ripe given noisy
greet well-fed defilement state of together
at night to oars tells a teller
horns ripple it
pastry a fond biting untamable money
peeling off one mealtime mischief
avoiding forgiving it
something burnt
this mixture susceptible to perforation
bends groan a dealer
one that's easy being big
desirable horseman a ship of sharing
unmoved seductively to
induce born assertion
war of words covered with handbag
the genitals
one small-eyed salad full of springs
overmuchness lasting to go that
sting talkative
wordbook's black of very roar

sharp-sighted to many-branched
playful as lasting
if consolation equipped to rouse
over rawhide or consisting bowlegged
expounder seeks the lamentable
(one busy space of relating)
open-end-up full fist to take steam
asking argues the stump comfortable
shaped with jeers hems a cushion
following stiletto "bearded but bold"
scorching with cavernous stake
to crown one branded
causes sweat to bruise an eye
visible coming brink
runaway lounger sweet bit's shade
innocence equipped and oil
still useless prime in entertainment
wifeless feet downgrade
forehead after dead-end arrogance
to repel
money with talk
a ram or union irksome welcoming
effort holes the morrow
enjoying damage
ambush passage clear
catch it or extract leave peak
thievery gewgaws
(or nonsense icon)
torn gynophile notice chaser brine as ointment
pitiless superfluity
speaker marks favour promises both
(reading must always be questions)
or wreath tattooed
darts much greedily
disentangled fact *vernacular*

Paper Sections   for Jane Creighton

Exits more attended than entrances for years now. The light fades
(oh yes) into night beat. Jackal harness, a double, please. Shoe
spectrums to remember by the ultimate platform twist. On whose
knees? Suede's not to soften any fall. Apart, her fingers frame the
trajectory of "become." We *are* the visuals, words have been before
us. Tell me. Lead into gradation, hang the hat on retro, hold onto
the door frame. Portability sinks from sight. To wander is a luxury
not stilled. Silk always slides downwards best. Advantage first
speaker. Streets are there with or without notice and shades align
shadow (only). Our attention is attracted now distracted by the
results of situations out of our control. What we see is carnage. In
differing locales evidence's out of tact, water, shovels, hope. Some
boxes were opened. P(l)ans flash, nothing in them. Generations of
objects collapse toward someone (else) if not us. Details don't mis-
lead. They follow main facts. Knowing why to write's different
from despair or running.

The outline differs sharply from month to month neither coming
to rest, nor departing, though this can't serve or be described as
territory to crowd the case. Voice, not statement may be concen-
trated on but the latter holds, deploys a view. Canny if resistant
combinations surrender pleasure. The tongue still gives what the
"I" holds back. Veins in a leaf, blast as a plan not to wake up to
much. Slip into the night. Irregular moments of non-interference
resist complaints. Patches splurge diagonally and lift-off into the
rubbish bin. Moving vehicles form the rehearsal of how we really
perceive all the time (not just sight, but sixth sense, too). Join
nothing, remember all the "seem to's" in a frame. Money on it.
Chequered is a portrait, suggestion isn't math, our "monsters" are
among us. Do we begin or end with flowers growing in both (ver-
tical) directions? Papyrus beat. Invasions mark our works (gone)
wrong.

A planned aracade rises only as far as the eyes can see. Fold the linen, not the spoons (legs bend to curl in pairs) to reflect graciousness. The pannicle holds to the knife's edge, flowers beyond, drooping. Landscape here is blurred by wind and more immediate concerns. Seasons tune the clock. Snuff performance art isn't beyond question. Spin the stop to go (dictates a quickness akin to sleight-of-hand). Quisquous if anything else. She looked at him in the chair, on the road, at desk. Hours of how many breaths in and out together. Shut the door. Open the book. Each year contributes to a curve in a letter of one's signed name.

Kathleen Fraser

from: when new time folds up

understood and scrupulous

I would have stayed at home as   rehearsal
if a bystander plated in gold,   food
understood and scrupulous among
metal bowls, but a doctor goes
to the Gymnasium where scale is   in key
brick to the heart and air com-
pletely empties itself, without
gender'd regard, thus I tried
my luck as "you", in neutral,
running with you as we talked,
inside the blue grape hyacinth
where nature reproduces its   represses
mechanical force, *rughetta*
wild in tomb grass,

a certain uneven panic

After tomb grass resistance, the occur-
ence of retinal loss, health sections
every Monday yet many coming into focus
of rue, woe, looking sideways, sidereal
normalstrasse, even hearing the gate
bang shut they could not give up where
truck beds beckon, it is such a one in
skirt length, heartbeat crumpled neatly
on white card, leather shoes with-
out pain, your yellow swimsuit dream
pinned on paper head-to-toe, retinal
crosswords, a certain uneven panic in
the presence of marble force, meat's
possible greed,

under us

old movie
dubs

girlfriend's wheelchair, gathering combs

Panned wide to shut door, soundtrack
gritty, moved camera slowly, returning   behind
tried not to weep while working, denied   you
all comfort of bread, backward zoom to
youthful self in camp (dream's concen-
tration excrement gone out of control,
skull with your number), wake up,
"Come forward five at a time", a little
speed now, danger over your shoulder, no   *Berlinerstrasse*
eating scenes, girlfriend's wheelchair,   scissors
gathering combs, your original murder
plot withdrawn, "*non così, non così*" (not
like that), in white collar, camera
forward, open,

from: Wing

I. The Underdrawings

The New comes forward in its edges in order to be itself;

its volume by necessity becomes violent and three-dimensional
and ordinary, all similar models shaken off and smudged

as if memory were an expansive thick creamy paper and every
corner turned now in partial erasure,

even bits of pearly rubber, matchstick and lucent plastic
leaving traces of decision and little tasks performed

as if each dream or occasion of pain had tried to lift itself
entirely away, contributing to other corners, planes and
accumulated depth

•

the wing is not static but frayed, layered, fettered, furling and
stoney

its feathers cut as if from tissue or stiffened cheesecloth
condensed in preparation for years of stagework

attached to its historic tendons; more elaborate
the expensive ribcage, grieving, stressed, yet

marked midway along the breastbone with grains of light

•

there are two men, they are tall men, and they are talking softly
among the disintegrating cubes

II. First Black Quartet: Via Tasso

A cube's clean volume
its daily burnt mark
backward into match
day's oxygen, common
the remaining light
nothing changed yet
have a way of crash

shatters and reassembles
The New is used and goes
sticks one struck at each
pinched breath and nerve
bricked-up Now melt with
he persists as does pain
ing in on you, swimming

through matter heart
are two men turning
that one particular
to unfold in expand
stars: "that which
improvised on deep
picking, pecking at
sent to tell us what

rate in each cell There
their limit of blanket
evening appears in reds
ing brilliant traces or
is known to us" or just
kitchen floor meanwhile
our skins ghost or angel
we didn't want to know

III. Wing: Via Vanvitelli

It can happen that the intoxicating wing will draw the mind as a
bow   The cubic route of wing falls backwards with light
leaking through at the edge   The cube is formally particular
and a part of speech and lost   it looks for like kind,
regardless of function, and attempts to replace itself   The
square root of anything captures and holds, seeming to be final,
and we are grateful   We see the delicate marks along the
feather and we follow, now to define or depict the outskirts of
meaning   A plume of smoke or any of the growths which cover
the bodies of birds   To form a model of the wing's surface,
the cube arrives on a day called "the darkest day"   Its
likeness consists of strength, atonality, pigment, emptiness and
shafts partly hollow   I put my mouth just at the opening where
a steel edge gives way to an angle   from which light emerges
along its soft narrow barbs   If the wing had a voice it would
open through a shaft   *I am not of that feather*

X. Vanishing Point: Third Black Quartet

forward edge itself to be volume by necessity as if partial erase

edge itself to be volume by necessity as if partial erase   other

itself to be volume by necessity as if partial erase   corners

to be volume by necessity as if partial erase   planes

be volume by necessity as if partial erase   accumulate

volume by necessity as if partial erase   depth

by necessity as if partial erase   condensed

necessity as if partial erase   in

as if partial erase   preparation

if partial erase   stagework

partial erase   historic

erase   tendons

of   elaborate

pearly   ribcage

lucent   marked

decision   midway

and   with

little   grains

tasks   of

of   light

pain   talking

had   softly

tried   among

to   disintegrating

lift   cubes

to lift   the

tried to lift   falling

had tried to lift   wing

pain had tried to lift   will

of pain had tried to lift   draw

tasks of pain had tried to lift   the

little tasks of pain had tried to lift   mind

and little tasks of pain had tried to lift   as

decision and little tasks of pain had tried to lift   a

lucent decision and little tasks of pain had tried to lift   bow

itself the wing not static but frayed, layered, fettered, furling

Lisa Robertson

from: Debbie: an epic

Hello nurses of words flattened as if

pronominal and parthenogenic

at the ordinary site of desire

striate light articulates the spurious

clacking of thought private justice cuts

lozenges into the blue your sewn lips

blent with the obfuscating grief of dun

grasses bent into themselves far phalanx

I speak to judge crimes of filiation

as hard sky spent cancelled horizon

my own mouth barking perhaps I am

unmentionable ticking against the

dark adjacency of prose lovely home

of gods and punctuation I say this

against the long and burning hills in the

slatey cold of debt

Dark artemis's division unpractised

splits into the staccato glamour of

february trickles lurex through the

arbitrary and distant apple tree

a girl's hard russet lace — it is the dreamt

world it is the buckled marsh hawked rhythmic

I see girls who as if armed and in

formation one figure seated and one

other standing — or two seated love

approaching — flaunt the pliant display of

tenderness

        others folding clothes one slight

ly bent to place her folded garment her

companion turning around ribboned

thigh to watch her bend compel you to enter

those rooms

        another will want to dream just

of those animals associated

with deities or Queens yet still display

the abstinent charm of insouciant

Venus (Venus after Venus stepped

out)

      some are called sweetheart and polish the

sexual lens as if it were a blurred

age

one's exact rage ranks an acrid point

Nouns and nerves decay sluices imply

honey or grease of light wrecks to frilled rust

equivocal as certain clocks trees die

hello nurses of clinical distance

with irony antiquity salts thee

How to Judge:

To those whose city is taken give glass
Pockets. To those whose quiver gapes give Queens
And pace their limbs with flutes, ropes, cups of soft
Juice. To those whose threshold vacillates give
That bruise the dust astonished. To falling
Heroes give raucous sibyl's polished knees.
To those who sip nectar give teeth. And if
They still sip nectar — give green chips of wood.
To swimmers give clocks or rank their hearts
Among new satellites as you would
Garbo's skint lip. To scholars, give dovecots.
To virgins, targets. Justice has nothing on them.
Virgil, sweetheart, even pretty fops need
Justice. If they think not let creditors
Flank them and watch their vigour quickly flag.
To exiled brides give tiny knives and beads
Of mercury then rob them of prudence
For prudence is defunct. To those who fist
Clouds, give powder. And if their sullen
Wallets flap, give nothing at all. Still
I have not addressed lambent fops
Swathed in honey, the stuttering moon,
Martyrs, Spartans, Sirens, Mumblers, Pawns,
Ventriloquists — or your sweet ego.
The beloved ego in the plummy light
Is you. When I see you in that light
I desire all that has been kept from me:
Etcetera. For you. Since your rough shirt
Reminds me of the first grass
Pressing my hips and seed heads
Fringing the sky and the sky
Swaying lightly to your scraped
Breath, since I hear
Panicked, my sister calling,
Since the gold leaves have all

Been lost, and you are at least
Several and variegated
I toss this slight thread back.

The beloved ego on cold marble
Blurs inscription. Dear Virgil
I think your clocked ardour is stuck
In the blue vein on my wrist. It stops
All judgement.

Marjorie Welish

Twenty-three Modern Stories

Perpetually roughed up
by the dawdling, blushing drone of an airplane,

"the viola with a restrained, sometimes" restringing
made the plunge

upon these planks
because of all the shores that must be visited.

"...and continuities, whose intersections"
spreading hot wax

on privation
and on the phrase "this text",

united once again,
are inescapably drawn toward the open door.

The bells have ceased altogether.
"The air bit hard and cold"
spaced in such a way as to make a triad
of arrangements thus:
old and tired star, guitar and protean
interdisciplinary soprano.

Crude Misunderstandings

Hair dyed black signifying the dogmatically youthful...,
and the evidence of intent

                     falls through the concept
in Picasso's rendering —

a kind of ultimatum of the much-extolled chiaroscuro
falling against the nose.

A torrential chiaroscuro to be thought about
or thought with:

                  as the intentional digestive of planes
contrariwise, her head opened out
                      like a parking garage.

Or a ruler with an orb.
A commandment no less unconditional
                   than pervasive space.

Call the space cloven by any distinction
axiomatic. Dye it black.

A vacant lot makes things pleasant.

Opera

It will have been
                      phrased in tauromachy
to cause people long-lasting pain.

Pulp and paper, the embodiments.

And in our restatement, in the scraped surface which
infuriated the subtle theorist,
                                mention is
growing pale as death, mention is enumerated.

It might have been
                        "the rubbing together of membranes"
in faces modulated through demonstrable use, tempting you
to agitate for
                  the right-hand edge left free —
and beneficial leaves.
                          Improving intelligibility, he moved further away.
By analogy, the rational cosmos.

To agitate for wax
                      which when rubbed
                                            as antihistamine
                    and most prolific spacing
cherished use
                of beautiful yellow gold
                                            insight
and prefigurement of beneficial chemistry.

It will have been a serious pursuit by aerial railway
swirling towards him.

An elevator raised by twelve columns
inscribes a place within a system
of urban agora
and superlatives sailing into our harbor.

Later we shall annoy our plants of heaviness, of lightness,
and we shall slide the gate of contemplative elevator to refer to
something
purchased
in a pleasantly static pursuit of experience.

Macbeth in Battle

"Let's get married." "That's False."
"Not unmarried," she estimated.

Redness is whimsical or whitened. "I wonder
where my wallet is?" is not a question

but an implicit temptation trafficking
in interrogatives. Adam and Eve

encumbered.
                    Between languages

subsisting on value, and modernism.
The idea of gray is not a true copy.
                                    "Don't!"

as a bridle for packages intimidated
amid prehensile pathways.

"What's the manner with you?"
                              "Ready, or not!"
if you rotate the letter "N"

in your dialect of mathematics. And on a dark night,
bridle, strap, leash, vanilla, are celebratory.

Imagining vanilla, the reliable confection
luckily aestheticized, we are tempted to say,

chasing ethics
after surgery.

Using clues: it is raining, it is not raining. Do not eat
                                        knives frozen.
"Excuse me?"

Do not eat peas with a knife, knives.

                              "Excuse me?"

                                        In brain areas,

"RAW" in neon
making "WAR" —

                    Or else! —

                              in physical interference

yet non-contradiction
mentions why.

Situation

                                    Failing this zig-zag (composed of
smaller zig-zags) while caring for chaos
are properties "less necessary." Nevertheless,

Nevers is failing part of his chest
                                    running out of the house
sequentially. Non-sequitur made by that.
                                    And she

whose syllables went saline, is unthought
or thought to be between mental states,
through which a sieve through which she drew a sieve
of disinformation,
                        pamphlets, and etc.
                                    (Subsequently repeated
tryst, heavily indebted
to a wall or to a wealth of adjacent method
for her whose personal history went saline among the pharmaceuticals
and sometimes tearful.)

And sometimes these seeming advantages fade
into face that is harbinger of extraneousness.
                                    Face related to a
lack into which a naturalism casts a few
                                    — the film is about the lack
of map, of mapping German onto French
fixity of the sign, through which reading himself satisfactorily went
into overdraft.
                        Unthought to be between mental states.
                                    And she,
attributing locutions, kept after.

Of a sequence unthought through a sieve
of disinformation

        in paper, half a mind to

                    up-end pocket money.

Negativity, the architect of,
would have something discontinuous to say.

Barbara Guest

Red Lilies

Someone has remembered to dry the dishes;
they have taken the accident out of the stove.
Afterwards lilies for supper; there
the lines in front of the window
are rubbed on the table of stone

The paper flies up
then down in the wind
repeats repeats its birdsong.

Those arms under the pillow
are burrowing arms they cleave
at night as the tug kneads water
calling themselves branches

The tree is you
the blanket is what warms
snow erupts from thistle
to toe; the snow pours out of you.

A cold hand on the dishes
placing a saucer inside
her who undressed for supper
gliding that hair to the snow

The pilot light
went out on the stove

The paper folded like a napkin
other wings flew into the stone.

Wild Gardens Overlooked by Night Lights

Wild gardens overlooked by night lights. Parking
lot trucks overlooked by night lights. Buildings
with their escapes overlooked by lights

They urge me to seek here on the heights
amid the electrical lighting that self who exists,
who witnesses light and fears its expunging.

I take from my wall the landscape with its water
of blue color, its gentle expression of rose,
pink, the sunset reaches outward in strokes as the west wind
rises, the sun sinks and color flees into the delicate
skies it inherited,
I place a scene there from "The Tale of the Genji".

An episode where Genji recognizes his son.
Each turns his face away from so much emotion,
so that the picture is one of profiles floating
elsewhere from their permanence,
a line of green displaces these relatives,
black also intervenes at correct distances,
the shapes of the hair are black.

Black describes the feeling,
is recognized as remorse, sadness,
black is a headdress while lines slant swiftly,
the space is slanted vertically with its graduating
need for movement,

Thus the grip of realism has found
a picture chosen to cover the space
occupied by another picture
establishing a flexibility so we are not immobile
like a car that spends its night
outside a window, but mobile like a spirit.

I float over this dwelling, and when I choose
enter it. I have an ethnological interest
in this building, because I inhabit it
and upon me has been bestowed the decision of changing
an abstract picture of light into a ghost-like story
of a prince whose principality I now share,
into whose confidence I have wandered.

Screens were selected to prevent this intrusion
of exacting light and add a chiaroscuro,
so that Genji may turn his face from his son,
from recognition which is here painful,
and he allows himself to be positioned on a screen,
this prince as noble as ever,
songs from the haunted distance
presenting themselves in silks.

The light of fiction and light of surface
sink into vision whose illumination
exacts its shades,

The Genji when they arose
strolled outside reality
their screen dismantled,
upon that modern wondering space
flash lights from the wild gardens.

Winter Horses

placed two sticks upon a dazzling plate
unlike feudal wars you remember
their saying she is stalking
and the fortifications are blocked
abruptly they held their breath until it froze.

carpeting the greensward a foil of sunset
"idyll of the kings" and shut the moat;
did not forget the promised tawny
situation of splendor.

again twists in the passage
or is it rhythm overturned;
to regard moodily a cask something
borrowed or fable stuck the snow

ii

sea grey cold a door one boulder
slams another.
              instantly footprints
in the sand corner.

    grief spell was thought something else
records what was cried out.

the shrived warm
              turns into serpent
                    are
no kingdoms
              is grass.

iii

winter
you know how it is *la gloire!*
they bring you a fig dish.
the dead in white cotton.
fleece on the platter.
wind crept
the white shoat and buried;
the cramped space ran
out of breathing.

iv

bars of snow lanced the brightness
crippled windows flung

lute with two notes unevenly.

ice breaking and noise
envelops sobriety.

slice of boot on the frayed sylph

came out of dazzlement into
fisheries was intended.

Grace Lake

Ordered into Quarantine

You have told me & in the telling have placed yourself above me as
my keeper
this lacks voice positively, though your one word devastated me
I do not therefore, following you, fill in the space or watch it for,
aware of the material nature of this structural exercise which has now
become a gratuitous act, falling into exercise, you annihilated me.

It is a pity that you took my body seriously, for what fears were yours
I have raced around myself like a maypole in the act of self
strangulation
what a twisted girl you were you might have sighed before you popped
me into the oven having broken me over your knee like a long
french loaf.

But plaited! That calmed me. Any threads in threes. Army blankets
fulfilled a purpose, or stars scratched onto a stone floor with the
heels of my shoes
or splitting matchsticks with a pin, an economical trick, who
would have thought
that would have proved useful, and to remember it in a
chamber airy and unearthly light if a blue butterfly flew out I could
nip its wing

In one bite feed on butterfly's wing by split match light & all for silence
for the lovely long life of limitless silence for nothing but wind, sun
& bird song

twelve to midnight

would my use of language be queried as characterizing one dispossessed
greeted by 'we are english', man, woman or child there is no one to ask.
senses locked, implying intelligence as one that interprets &
                                          articulates them.

a quieter place which jolts a memory of being slapped, & lying
                                          under the bed
with a book. Tyranny is nothing to brag about. Victory seethes, bed
                                          springs make dull music

as rivers flow by brown industrial landscapes a mattress fell over a fall.
they don't know. there is no such thing as common intelligence.
                                          there is no intelligence.
there's an anti-fascism and an anti-semitism and that is all, anything
i did wrong was potentially anti semitic, anything. i could not speak.
treated as a walking joke. family lore. i grew consciously

stunted, seated on the bottom step whenever they called to visit us.
struggling home from school with stomach ache, reluctancy at its
                                          limit. No God.
Yes God. And never breathe 'maybe' because it presents a sexual
                                          possibility.
And I won't talk. And i won't talk. And i won't talk. So i watched it.

as it was being played. i replaced all the receivers which were left dangling.
calk if you like calk caltanissetta it is impossible to ask a question
                                          based on a stated premiss
that without a palette art exists in a lively though elusive manner
the risks of surrendering too experiential
if you like chalking on stone the truth has always been a point not two
i didn't scratch stars onto a stone floor with the heels of my shoes

i had no shoes. my feet were filthy from walking on city pavements.
they were walking to italy. to caltanissetta. for the colour of
twinkling sulphur. could not be explained as a lemonade frock

locked shamefully away from dress to a doing nothing but dancing that feeling contorted to an old nothing wrong, time unpunctured by positioning he must have had fun. there is no room for anything to be taken from. mine was mind. long roads up into the mountains in the centre of a city where a plum tree was tantamount to an indiscretion. a clutch of chapters follows on the subject of religion, for that racial stigma that has congratulated the most lofty minded of litterateurs into semi-conscious blood libel. for hands held apart in sheffield.

Silk & Wild Tulips

Afraid of my father's power the object speaks country does it concur
Entering this petrification, perforce the accident is indicative it is
A report, repeated pondering fall, a petition, a portrait I would not bear
A portrait of throated wires through blood
It is demanded of me that I die having neglected my duty.

I read of women who have been found disregarding class, the heavy book
Bearing the sombre tone, we anyway tremble whilst we are broken down.
What is love? o what is love? the tip of a tongue, a silk white dove.
that will not fight and is crushed by speculation, a sinful breast
Cleansed, the surprising lightness in weight, the emphasis returned to
Provocation, that is the dead weight, that we cannot speak until
                                        spoken to
And divided by omission are invited to attend to the traffic signals,
                                        obsessively
Indicating slips don't for one second imagine that I am in the least
                                        oppressed.

Prussian myzi, if only I could wait for your magnesium blue to hover
stone by stone over the shark finned ground, resonations floor me
I am told that I have reinvented my history, these fakes that have
Drifted by desire rather than by noble patriotic inclination, to be
                                        told this
Frozen kiss is a parasite berry that grows and governs our merriment
That we fall to habitude unaged & are given brown cloaks for
                                        mourning
To circle the lotus that catches the tip of the dragonfly's wing
And burning it into fruition find an exhaust pipe carved in braille
The war continues to char the air with shot speech,
Theses are buried or placed on parole for comparing the language
                                        of war & of peace

We are old with the sound of horsehair, the most beautiful poems
                                        speak to us
Yet we know they were written in the wrong country at the wrong time
When poets were forced to cross borders despite euphorbia
Unknown by date and place, the ocean resented them when uttered
A mumbled ocean slapped to make an eternally recorded impression
When we slapped the ocean the beach was too large for reality
And petty dictatorship of relative supernity returns to the bearer
that streaks green across black meadows sky scumbled blue quaternity
the reduction by not first dissolving perhaps never dissolving
what change has no time to name its causes, its reasons
for not reading paintings as though they were rule books,
Believing themselves to be needy some make a lifetime of need
That can be expected to fall by the covers of contentment
And settling that, progress through a sequence of tranquil passages
Minute squares some crossed some kissed by stars and shells
Open'd by background loss, closed by measured step,
Around the fountain the old men slept, the women deep in the heart
                                        of roses rouges foncés,
And the chimney sweeps wept until they discerned that their tears
                                        had created ink
To tell of squares of blue & finely pointed moons, silhouetted cats'
                                        upturned tails
Catching at the lunatics they promised the coals would glow
Memories of tail coats arranged around angel pie & a tankard of
                                        stiff pheasant feathers.

by gardenias i cannot telephone
am excluded by the young racist
who cuts wires but won't run from me
so that i can stay with these gardenias
where voices fall pull down my colours
using race to materialize my gardenias
into shivering apologies for absence
a clever poetess would flee i am a potato
my clothes are made of potatoes
and you expect me to leave these gardenia clouds
that become blue for my chalk face
is greeting a pink too true to be lilac
too white to be fading too scarey to be stem
of tulip in the deafening scrim
yellow silk your heart darkens

Concilia

eyelash once eleven jonquil cibachromed en route
washington vacuous quay point sizzling palermo
messages visited square bank ochre charged by bolt
magnet, curtsey, falling out, back room rat:
white sliced delivery, spanish cake shop windows,
tiled frames fused infantry, grille, behind a face
a ransacked library, daubings, bricked out.
descriptive psychology dents & is reinforced
unglobed throat, fascistic debasement a la mode
grained in wheaten filings, securely modern ode.
to a river, refusing filtering piston'd sing, verge
it is not the thing it is the representation of the thing
the idea as god and gods and not a sensible sense of what could
cohere without damaging itself, as an idea. not to be
cheapskated, for personal reasons, learning excludes sex
if hell is another's sky, it was an obedient moment.
sanctioned who is not the licentiate of magister logos.
reactionary creation of familiar narrative, self serving.
tempting to embarrass and then dress in embarrassment
remarking in copyright ISBN'd on fictionalized naked emotion
encouraged dulcamente to change that to terror, scattered,
shadows, behind a hammed production of a national condition.
speechless, open mouthed, tongueless fish. Felicitations.

She Walked where she should have stood still,
or edging slightly, morose, if not moribund and there
she stood too far from the yorkist, to be of much use
she knelt by the casement it took her ages
her legs were too long they had been part sawn off
it was cheaper than extending the length of her rest
but he waited, as only the dead could.

the day it was dull and as silent as dullness
without any breeze to lend to this nullness
numbly did old Flem bleed with a fullness
to blench oaken gall into satin and all
the works at Tyre were appointed to dress
sixteen pieces of what were the best
crimson modules, to be routed, by errantine hergest.

finja and minja were chomping on apples
not yet incorporated into the box
break time was over, short break as always,
they continued to whiten the winnings of hergest
and that is why, lambkins, to this very hour
in the even grey drab uneventful power
when your energy overbrooks the salt will go dour...

Caroline Bergvall

Of Boundaries and Emblems,
from The Underlip

Having Spent Much Time In Such Manner Crouching In On
Myself And With The Ivy Infiltrates, Less Pensively Than Out Of
Halted Feel Across Networks We Outgrow And Beyond The
Outposts, Each Extended Against The Impasse, The World But
Round For Brute Supplies, Walk Into The Solid Seas.

Along Clear Dry Avenues, The Light Falls Flat. Coming Out In
The Afternoon, Momentarily Blinded By The Day, The Wind
Sweeps The Streets Clean In Violent Jerks Like A Sense Of Time,
Brings In A Stench Of Debris And Wastage,
     You Say Ah: Will We Ever Be The Same, Form Is Cold Where
Growth Was Resinous, Large Hollow Bodies Roll Over In Waves
Of Decidability.

Still Calling Across The Lines Of These Retractile Sceneries,
Always Surprised With The Peculiar Responsiveness Of Their
Magnetic Overload, Unfolds Noise And Parasitical Invasions,
     Where Heat Spreads From Lip To Lip In The Sparking
Undergrowth And A Volatile Sense Of Unreality Drifts, Impeding
The Drainage Of Excess, Travels Are Slow, Weighed Down By
Aches That Shoot Into The Spine.

I Work My Way From Shadow To Light To Matter, Still Seem To
Be Coming Endlessly Through The Slackening Resistance Of
Corroded Speech Material, Mouths Fantastic And Red That
Would Spit Me Out Completely Of Subliminal Terrains, Great
Holes Of Silence Great Caves Of Worship, Days And Years Go By
The Crack That Runs Along The Ceiling, The Lines And Names
Into The Walls, This Emblematical Surface Making Me Weak

And Tentative: Words Come Apart In Sounds, You Pick Morsels
And Consonants From Between My Teeth, If The Flesh Be
Framed In A Series Of Free Convulsions, What Could We
Possibly Keep And Recognize?

By Evening We're Inconsolable. Having Reached This Far, Bent
Over Tables Of Effervescence Within The Claustrophobic Bounds
Of The Yellow Foreground: Art Has Kept Us High And Separate,
Hard In Pointed Isolation, Forever Moved By The Gestures Of Its
Positions And The Looseness Of Even That: Now Vexed And
Irritated, Still Plotting Endless Similitudes: We Trip Over Things:
Strain To Extricate Ourselves From Closing Borders:

What There Is To Learn From The Fortitude Of These Aggressive
Plants, Keeping A Clear Head Arbitrarily, Hard To Break The
Paraded Sequence, Easy To Get Lost, Merely Easy To Give Up :
Dreams Get Heavier : Reality More Sudden On Bad Days The
Wind Carries Dust Particles Burn Tiny Holes Into Our Clothes,
Times Of A Serpent's Tail And The Depths Of My Artificial Eye :
Consider The Dark And The Expanse : From The Stupor Of This
Third Nature : The Second Urban : The First Nonexistent.

from Strange Passage

FOURTH TABLEAU

VOICE 1
If to belong (is to erase) is to appear, then to pronounce the currents-ah which search the body mass and caught us speechless and were gone. This excitement this sudden rash this unexpected full view. As we slowly turn: from sleep to motion as we come to pass: from semi-visible to nonchalantly here.

THE CHORUS BREATHES IN DEEPLY

VOICE 4
If to be recorded is to be seen, across inflected speech, were you even there crossing the pier up the landing board, were you even there crossing the pier up the landing board.

THE CHORUS BREATHES OUT

VOICE 2
Cutting corners say: aha! while the open secrets that guard and transform, grab you by the hair, pull me out of somnolence in a cloud of wet dust, thin mud, and the piercing cries of night birds. Precipitation: violent passages: from which we each emerge: rending: stuffed: awkwardly shaped by the heat of such and such a system.

THE CHORUS BREATHES IN DEEPLY

VOICE 1
If to be exposed is to occur: in deposits of vision: in a general situation: in a specific capacity, defined by loose disguise and composite transformations, in pouches of air where flies, ash, particles of undigested matter confusedly recall a hidden overwhelm upsets and nourishes the unfolding flesh.

THE CHORUS BREATHES OUT

VOICE 4
Ah letting hot dextrous manipulations investigate areas of concealed sedation, pockets of flatulent mind redressed by high decorum and the painted splendour of high eyebrows.

THE CHORUS BREATHES IN DEEPLY, BREATHES OUT WITH A LOUD, SHORT:
Ha!

VOICE 1
Excavate the drumming breath: the ha ha loud: the tactile plenty of days for fear of losing all direction.

THE CHORUS
Ha!

VOICE 1
Trail shadows loud and heavy: release oh stretch of transformation.

THE CHORUS BREATHES IN DEEPLY

VOICE 1
Flaunt: flourish: differentiate: is the starting block. Richly carved is the open vastness of deserted architectures in islands pushed back by a sense in time. Ornamented gestures that reach vegetal proportions, rot back down to the ground and rise again. Force the language swells! grows, gorges itself with exaggerated overwhelm. Language of this fruitful grasp, this persisting sense, pressing measures out of opening creases. Touch ground, folds, fine attire, replete appearances: touch ground, bead-clustered agitation.
What I seek fluent, brutal, resonant, caught in the peripheries, peeling senselessly, yet forming sounding across this vast cavern of shapes, derailing I pronounce: that to plant teeth vigorously

brings conviction to this peculiar articulation, this pondering sound, this developing heat, like slow events between us, the troubling virtual, the multiple and seamless. Breathe in: dilating unpronounceables, breathing out your ha ha loud, shiver, shaking the bells in cybershape, saying breathe out the contortions of the position I'm in might eventually break into song breathe in would shape and multiply breathe out would not catch you unawares breathe out my shedding skin exudes: an acrid smell breathe out that lifts passes of change from torrid material breathe out walk the mind feet deep breathe out from disappeared from tired constructions breathe out to fecund diversity breathe in if one step fully breathe out.

Ah: first there was the Real: everything be: larger than be: and separate: that cracks under the icon visibility of its very distractedness.

Might come to lean toward the more: flourishes from unpredictable roots Of forms and temper: of untold plenty: of necessary presence: of live cohesion of magnetic ground: Absolute when walked upon, when rested on.

Flutter and run: Find and let go.

(Pause then slowly)

THE CHORUS

Strange passage ... avid mouthful ... crush a plum caress a curl ... a shedding skin ... a healing state of ha.

Fiona Templeton

from Arachne, from Ovid's Metamorphoses

God the grape treads the guarding girl.
God the mount tramples half a man from her.
All foreign framed and divided within:
creepers poke open her warp and her web chokes closed.
(She has grassed on the vices of great ones.)

The other (spoken as intelligence, that is the second person
but defaced as mirror's futures) ripens poison envy.
Will not second the fair first.
She rips the fabric fraught of crimes of god.
Her own box-wood instrument of bias
Delivers three blows to the temple of the girl.

Whose great heart brookes it not.
She weaves her throat a noose.
Such end denies the immortal other, who
stops her plummet, damning: Hang alive in fault.
And your children, and your race.

I cut my hair. Nor smelt nor heard. Ate Eat me.
I seemed all breast. Nor thought.
Needed no legs for lying but fingers to pet
a new web spelling in me, a lock stroked out,
my spider-thighed thread of unbroken throat.

Part of an ongoing "translation"

Melanie and Andy
on reading a text by each (Melanie Neilson and Andy Levy)

Who, me? You, who? I don't, wait, let me remember. Or anyone, or else, if untrue, and defined by words that correspond to no reality but that of corresponding to no reality, and this being being. And that being harder to remember, especially as I saw or felt it, or as you saw or felt it, because the words are yours. Because the words are yours I have never been there. Harder than speaking but this is the place. Never been polite before, that is, never part of society. Name, then place. I won't go there and that sounds too like to be. Already you are both in America and more particularly anywhere that the mind's body or the eye's mind's body, meaning plan, can be in the mind.

You pull out your culture in the nature and one writes and one reads. The writer reads random measure and the reader follows as described, exactly. Which holds me far enough in, not to place but to displacement? Here in elsewhere is a pickup on a train, language in translation, collision on television. I'm not feeling myself. Your eyes are in moving heads.

Returning with memory or following towards yourself, your self is what begins, and *your* self begins in the centerline of the State highway. Here is the departure that is reached from what the journey will describe inside itself. The more I look the less I've found it, borders, stepping sideways, half-remembered because surrounding does not require entry. Goes without saying because how else would you have got there, more local than personal? You will put moving body together (later) from above, and *you* are too late, the way wishes compensate, and more old American language.

So I moved on too, to neither having begun-and-contained. In fact you are both moving at great speed, officially, thanks to me, on a train, a sort of place. I need you, not to see, more like a piano or an orange, any orange, though I'd prefer a local orange. Pianos are heavy. I look with civil eyes, hearted and handed.

And having arrived? The road is spoken already and *you* think you're where it's at, out from, personally speaking, though who runs the blood in your face but niceties of people as place? Further down the highway you stand looking down at nothing that can be held, again, a point of walking inside your thighs turning to face a new delineation, path that seems to answer unwillingly, over a turned shoulder, a body all along between the mouth and you, but mouth leading because ahead, to come, after, behind, here, a fence post, fields of result fastened around a great tree.

Where you are going is not but makes what you're making, the flat of your profile strokes, and stumbling helps your pig head find the center of a ditch, find how pigheaded, and remaining in the spoken ditch, that hearing after draws you on. Time is a smaller part of direction, before distance, and my having arrived, or closed the table, does not alter the noted coincidence, only the now remembered unnoted coincidence, a lot of green things on the table, and this couple picking each other up, including both pieces of writing, that is, my intention may not have been to alter, but there we were, nothing pure, I'm happy to say, or was happy to say, in the strongest terms possible, to a point; thence, to a point.

Down here in the ditch with me is another ditch. There is no way of knowing if the land is flat or hilly, or am I swimming? You describe the description, not the described. Other than is non-made, not unmade, at least, I hope I feel that I die *my* death. This is not a report of nature, but it is a report. This is not a translation of a name of a place on a board in a station in France. The name means the place, and to me it means where I'm going as well as where I'm staying, missing the boat and why. And the report, carried again, comes with me, as do yours.

Some points have names, Lovell's Southeast Corner, but whenever is lying and being, because this is not without us, nor our being without ourselves. And *your* place has been thrown away from the words of your being in the place, and from having been there a few drop heavily from your mind, and into place, like as I climbed and inside his thighs. And what have *I* made? A still life of a point not on the corner of anything, as if being without myself, dead nature, the worst of both non-worlds.

In living culture, sic, people dress as what they might have been and everything to see has been pointed at. What I'm pointed at is not but makes what I'm making, as long as I keep moving, as short as I stop crawling in the ditch. The ditch was outside of me but this new barrier is what I am outside of, a route really, only between you and what you'll contain by never climbing the fence. You only told so much, whether the ditch was the place for me or I was a person to be in a ditch. Did I choose to let you know how I felt about this ...accident, after all, or is culture how I feel about it?

So you swing (my impulse was to shout) around a fence post and see your name heading off. He's arguing and I recognize, presumably, myself. Don't make me leave, I'm nowhere anyway, locked in a transparent place, culture's otherness, moving. Your name leads you to a new iron pin placed there, presumably, for this purpose, to the point of beginning and containing, but this is not its own plan, but more ...local? (the marble floor), moral? (pretence), transcendent? (language). You, having retreated inside, sleep, celebratory, and *you,* more easily confused with me, because also absent, but having surrounded, let me in, that is, contain the possibility of passage (at last).

And if they knew each other really, not just on television, I mean in the movie, I mean on the train?

Paris-Boulogne train, September 1989

Human Non-Site

How I came back as the person who left, having lost elasticity, heirlooms and other proofs of existence, and by a quite different means of transport, substituting the purchase of bread for forms of politeness, of invisible recognition, only to find the stable door bolted to keep me on all fours, a safe bet with a name you'd choose sight unseen, a bit off, slightly ahead, being born because I liked it, the only way if brand name products satisfy all criteria for culture and all need, the application filled out with xeroxed answers, I mean they like one another, because the questions only address the outside of the buildings, of heads who admit it and are admitted, but who knows after that, well, who knows how? Take the Atlantic Ocean, the River Clyde, the English Channel and the Mediterranean Sea, what do you get, some careful crazy-paving you have to break up to put together, like shoes, pants, a body without a head, I mean my arms and legs like each other and write it down to sing it later, waiting for a coach in the middle of a field, a world in the middle of a house, sty in sleeve, head and tree, made and touched, being got? Got. Some places you have to be the way you are, aren't there, I can see them from here, nowhere unless there is more than one thing, maybe my getting it.

The jackhammers begin at nine. These people vote. Chocolate rocks come in sixpacks. Such sites. With the conditionality of bloom, far apart by transport following worm, but hugging on a folded, once smallest part. Who decides, what sticks, what to? Look down, born into armour, over silver bells and cockle shells, at least when crashing about for a big change, being the same as and turning into, just because what was born against showed up. The place of the change is apart from the place of the reason, that is, the reason the change was a reason, the reason the reason changed it, reasons a landscape apart.

"It" takes place. Comes out means something's out already. In the speech of armour, on entering the body, much good. Born against is cruised successfully, on the same stem. A knot could be a place, a secret could, or a projection on nature. All other tiny players produce secrets.

Definite isn't only, only here. From here what's seen has been before. So on the car, didn't even get in, a straddled skull bangs its way out enough to be seen on an internal security system blind but to this coupling, of an inferior internal security system not conscripted psychiatrically, couldn't get screwed, fought the wrong enemy, with its own improbable child. What turns on this sight-capacity we can only imagine, but who are we, but here you are, ricocheting in the supermarket aisles, looking behind you, but who are you whenever the clanged door works behind you and you call out as expected? Not far, a meeting, its moment, this is the one, among others (is this being unaware if I have to ask?), goes into a blast routine with DNA, RNA and getting the meat together, and multiplies. Obviously, those others, alone or safe, that is, defined, who-me or the ends of the earth, taking place to be around, however locally, meaning microhistory, can and did, a sigh of continuation, of privacy, of being in her seventies and tidying this here and that to herself. Equally composing, equally surrounded, a growing screen turns or is turned to whose invisibility or its own, to be got by, entering for the first time, the abated ends. On a corner at Airdrie Cross, the chain store didn't last, mockings meeting. Such ends are excited to emulation and difference, the loving manufacture of arms and their smuggle, a chip off. The new prisoners are slapped on your simultaneous plates, or so they claim when introducing at court, to the sceptically avid, our bashed baby, into that very flattering or defining sexual topography, vacuum-formed and blowing bubbles in self-defence. Here is baby's handkerchief, folded to hide the monogram that will allow your claim. Perhaps it bears more than one. Perhaps it is indecipherable. I will watch it turn you on, I'd like you to meet. It helps, and here, on your other plate, bursts the for of the against, if I fit.

What does it cost who to lock who in language? Look at it this way, inserted, nice to meet. Gravida zero, avoid the credits, miss the step, the ending. The image develops like writing a letter without an address. Be picked up, met out of fear, on a train, hiding the red carnation. Whip it out to an addressee among others, presto, spread on the knee, read, waved at the window to windows, as got. Help, you are being held by a wicked assumption in a high capital. You are not being held, as by a bridge, over a birth-canal, wherever and ever who, waiting for the and-then. In the act of wrapping or attaching a swell adrift from what started the difference to a majority minority, slipped already, floated, hooked on what it represents, represents three thousand francs, madame, a swell of caffeine, a slice of classism, a member of its thoughts. What is foreign? Gatecrashers perhaps revealed with the and-then to have feelings and the mobile home to be me, they look like as they lie by how I am along with myself for the ride, on the inside, an active pedestal not allowed however on the same bus or the same pay. Say the statue can win prizes standing on its head, say people pour drinks down its throat to cure their own thirst or stroke their own shoulder in admiration of the statue's patina, a puzzled rise at the rate of breathing together, wouldn't who okay, ring no bell, fight no superstructure? Who read the letter found in a drawer will not reply, an unchanged elsewhere when the writer against is around. Self-recognition is an inactive or tautological polis of what holds us together.

Finally, switch on sun in top corner of picture. Now compose only those elements not in yesterday's decisive mirror, and I couldn't do it without your today. Your soft person's protective outside interest and mine are what changed age. Is a car down to earth more than silent elsewhere outside? Software than hardware is that Moscow is Moscow and a woman is a woman even if you thought they were the same, or you seem to resemble then, a long time, no thread no mirror. Steed, campaign, presentation, picture on a wall, answer them all, fulfilling whose needs because only fulfilling whose needs, not in so many words but coming in her crisis of trust, other's war. The prisoners advise this coaxing and ant-like conservation of resemblance across time. Who is who to gainsay a desire to defend, not under attack but yet? Eeksy peeksy, pal; and the non-ulterior, the smile, the chest, the delicacy of object of mutual enclosure elicits the question of yesterday's picture, visible or no. Bodies orient in a convulsion of divination as in rods towards a decision hingeing on the sense born without, that folding makes alive. Not an abstract balance but what a good idea, in chains towards being near, pointing just so, now the landscape in a purely geometric sense and which house who doesn't go out of decide the painful extraction of myself, from who, from you, inter-section with who, for you, whoever you are, for all our sakes, sakes like selves. This is how the food is found, no similarity to playing husband and wife on a European train but non-repeating, joined for reasons, discipline maybe, transcendence preferably, the differ-ence between novelty and unfamiliar as an everyday guide to predicaments, syndromes, topographies of recognizing the unrec-ognizable, truth and love, that sort of thing. And so that I can know it, in the food is sought the internal image of this sort of thing, as my body comes back against the picture of a fool of a body that is raised against the skull on the car.

Le Cannet, September 1989

(I owe the title to Carl André who owes half of it to Robert Smithson.)

Fanny Howe

from: Democracy: Chapters in Verse

> *If you have no expectations, you can't be disappointed.*
> — a survivor of Hurricane Andrew

1

After the storm the word WATER kept rising
and circling the color oil.
The snow of the ocean blued and whirled.
There was water in all the machinery.
Waves knocked a water tower into a boat thrown off-course
by the hurricane. A ruined deck and dock, trees
uprooted from the heaving ground.

2

Gloved and cycling, the worker leaves the house.
His forehead is gleaming like David's.
The ground can hear his motions, the grass divides.
Pink hibiscus in the mist: for many like him all this
has been hellish. Compressed by the cosmos, not embraced,
he knows the dread that can't say yes.

3

It's as if money's eyes are located inside a pyramid.
Unfit for the rest of human habitation. Not like a cone,
generously spilling, he decides,
passing a blind couple walking, sighted child between.
Hard luck stories are never boring.

4

After a storm there's a powerless period, when the word
POWER keeps repeating, and when will the clock go on
in the kitchen and the trees finish falling in the mind.
He recalls his mother
whose days have the resonance of drums
played on the shins of a lazy teen. Her nouns
are thoughtless as shoes to be worn till the soles
of the feet show. To begin again where?
Near the pink dollop at the back of the tongue.

5

The playing field is disheveled.
His anger's target is on his way to a party
near the drive-by harbor slow-boated by boys
in motorized canoes. His power is out.
Only cars fathom the between, obsolete as soon as seen.
Nothing tech can stay: rust of entropy edges even
a bloated bike tire laid out on a stump.

6

The worker's mother was always seeking the problem
behind the fix
and wanting him to solve it. With thread on her lip
she, at home after work, nagged him.
Meanwhile an orderly twilight inks the twinkles
and the mathematics of stillness
is holiest when everyone is changing for bed, or in it.
If a star is in her eye, she knows the star
is finding itself, there, in her eye. Enlightenment
is a level without measurement.

7

The worker played king on a bike through seven gates
where trees lead to capitalist parties, cocktails
and the kitsch of four cultures. The maid
washed the dishes and spat in the chocolate.
Fill in the blank where that man stood
not a day earlier as Everylove to this woman
at the end of her bed. Her maintenance since then:
the wind, emptying — an emotion to lean on.
Often in her melon-yellow uniform
melancholy wouldn't quit her till she hit the kitchen
and the dishes waiting to pay her.

8

Summer of the linoleum tulips.
Storm entropied into drips. She will, for days
after the gale winds blow over, bear fruit
and bag her own vegetables. Friendship
she offered others into the moon-hours, drink from
supernatural grapes and potatoes.
Rubber slicked on asphalt under the branches,
saws attacked the remnants of trees. Her psyche cracked
where a mirror made the candle brighter.

9

She is making a cake in the post-storm kitchen.
Outside champagne rains air in a bottle.
Desire simulates fire as sure as she has heard a voice
in her ear call her. The head at her feet —
the eyes in her palm — the supplicant dishes look up —
indications of Saint Monica wanting to appear
in her consciousness. Ordinary time's daily prayer
for the conversion of workers to angels.
But only pure prayer makes the air into an ear.

10

After the storm, the long-limbed oak trees twist. Corkish.
They drank in kitchen wicker, and watched.
Are those half-people or chairs at a bar? He held her
ankles with his feet.
People are begotten from eternity, only to be returned.
And the animals of Paradise?
Let fortune smile on them! Or: send someone to burn
these monsters up. A person worthy of a sparrow's ashes.
Together one night they hosed down his anger, and learned
that a wound is only the edge of self-awareness.

***

16

She could have backed up into the target of his anger's belly
and done violence. Assassinate. One giant step
would accomplish it.
His arm even extended over her shoulder,
not interested in contact, colder than a barber
at Treblinka. He was the right temperature
for those who kill by proxy. But she believed
in the immortal soul and hesitated.
What if the rosary is a heresy?
What if the world is divine?
What if hell is a permanent state of mind?
What if the saints live in outer space?
What if a Jesus does too?

17

After the storm, the sun is drying seaweed,
winds dying over Toronto,

cloud formations gold as print.
On the West Coast
the sand has the hue of a burned lion.
Whispering sandmen say the hurricane is gone —
shelters for periwinkle and people — can be closed again.
And into the ears of babies, prayers
take a circular turn.

18

Scissors cut up the tree's meat.
Chickenish interior ripped by hurricane winds.
Everywhere people struggle
to be individuated in company. They pay for everything.
Sere leaves of August are used as window decorations.
Plates drip with oil like recreational vehicles
in the harbor. The temptation to poison
the plutocrats is a goal for the underling
to play bone with.

***

33

After the storm, a fragile boat, welded to a wall
of water, floats backwards over the grey water, with rain
attached like threads to a tapestry.
The statue of Lenin has fallen on its side
becoming a garden ornament after a storm.
And if this is a ballad, its refrain is secret.

34

Misery maintenance, cold pipe of the radiated
rain. Down to stone, gravel and ladder,
out of the kitchen window, she spoke of pastel water.
But what is it really? The orange is over the snack bar.
And tonight the sleepless hers will give away their slick
desires to illness, cramp, perverse renunciations
of the heart to others. It's a Via Negativa: no way EVER
to have both an honorable and youthlike power.

35

What if, she said to the man, *I never meet a worthy man?
And what if I really do die in the end?*

The Gerard Manley Hopkins in her thinking
made him listen. He was called outside to fix
a broken line, to get the lights going again.

36

I want the world to be good, is the only thing.

37

You have to bend the bitterness with markings
and tragic erotics, in order to get yourself straight again.
After the storm the earth is running down,
it's turned the entropy up. He sees
from the top of a pole that givers and payers are one
person. Takers and debtors are too.
Sins of criminals and assassins hold no candle
to the issue of justice which is also too big to see.

38

The technology of his tool makes a worker unable to murder
with it. Could a carpenter wound with a nail?
Is it supernatural if you can't put a name to a shadow?
Her questions kill his will to kill.
Telegraph, telegram, telephone —
three cruciforms declaring ALONE.
The man was hanging like an obsolete puppet, or
like the second to win. The wind pulls the strings.
And the lights go on.

39

Beside the mountain ocean, speed of snow
is the foam bubbling light, green.
The priceless wet-side
is like a benign wall through a tunnel
of appetites made lacy, and abstract.

THE END:

When she sees his eyes later — red and swollen
and faraway, she remembers the symmetry of the stars
at night, and whispers freely,
I don't know what to do with the poetry.
I don't know what to do with my body.
He tells her she has done it already.

Bernadette Mayer

from Moving

fear   sure   voice music   body   time   listen
being part. being trapped
being part being trapped   which is it?
   being trapped masculine
       should you be one
       should you be eight   one   eight
   anxious
       there's the woman   & there's the woman
       the frame of a woman
   rib is a frame
         filling station
      Rhythm break age water searching. Rhythm age
break water. Rhythm water searching.   Age water.   Water
break.   Break water.   Age searching.   Rhythm water.
   remember   positions
  remember what you saw
     seeing people in positions.   Remember what you
saw, people in positions.
           the round jungle
           jungle round
  the jungle   jungles filled
tumbling to one
     tumbling to see outside
hitting   hitting the wind
             the wind hitting
        who is the prince
       what is the prince
      the prince hears the music
      he hears it last
at the beginning
     the beginning over
laugh
      the scissors make sure

ground reverse   reverse ground
cabbie   a truck   comes out   the cab cabbie
emerges   indulgence comes out of the truck
other planted drops
drops, plant, drops, plant
young plant
young plants   I hear what they're saying
square and lucky, & believable
saddle
saddle the horses   horse's saddle
large drop   big drops
a large account
camera account   on cameras
the camera's down
down far enough
the reverse
face the camera
because
we've thrown it, the tough part
use it, we've thrown it, we've used it, throw it,
we've thrown it, used it
transition
the sea direct
the sea of white
the sea of organs
the sea of sympathy
wanted
at the head of the thought, a pin, a pin in the middle of
traffic, in traffic mind, a sea improve, in green, green
could improve, green will, a certain green will bend the king
a certain green will bend the king
king, bend.
jazz   lid   a mouth a covered mouth
a guy jack   wanted to cross
never crossed
realist, first   first to touch
first to touch plant
touch plant   touch exclusive plant

real plant

the expedition rose
the expedition crossed
dress of the expedition
share of the dress
piece of the holiday dress   but such stars,
they, those stars talk, go on, goes on,
& come level, came level, & slaves & companions,
level that their pistols, pistols play,
level pistols, aiming behind,

flowers
flowers screaming
flowers yelling, screaming
earnestly,
honestly blown
honestly blown aside
down side the mountain wheel, this is the wheel
down side the mountain wheel, this is the wheel, the wheel
giants came
giants lake, lake, & married
giants fade   giants fads,   always five,
when, then,   when down smiled,
when down smiled the beat   right almonds
when down smiled the almonds
almonds descend   almond down
descend her   on her   now
something loyal
some flower screaming
some fishing, & some loyal fishing
custom nothing
nothing season
the season's nothing
the season was evidence
move
move will plow,   did plow
did plow their turning   did plow their turning plow
their turning plow   did plow their turning plow share this

The Garden
for Adam Purple

Close to a house on a piece of ground
For the growing of vegetables, flowers & fruits
On fertile well-developed land
Is a delightful place or state, a paradise
Often a place for public enjoyment
Where grows the alyssum to cure our rage

Oriental night of the careless developers
Carpet of snow of the drugged landlords
Basket of gold the city's confused
Royal carpet of its bureaucracies,
Bored with bombs
Political ones of the complicated governments
Now stick up the very orb
For its non metal yet golden remains

Competing with the larval corn borers
The salried test-borers
Imminently lead anti-sexually down to the foundation
Of the annihilation
Of a circular garden in which live members of
The mustard family
The tomato or nightshade family
The poppy family
The geranium family
The aster family
The mint family
The thistle or aster family
The violet family (heartsease)
The lily family
The cucumber or gourd family
The rose family
The composite or daisy family
The parsley or carrot family

And other families
(I dont think the pokeweed family lives there,
It earns too little or too much money per year)

We are told to swallow not a rainbow
But like the celandine the juicy proposal
That the lemon balm of low income housing,
Applied like ageratum to the old Lower East Side
(As early matured as the apricot)
And probably turned by deeply divided leaves
Like a rape of grapes before it's all over
Into the poison tomato leaf of middle income housing,
Cannot coexist with the gleaming black raspberries
In an ancient abandoned place
Around Eldridge, Foresight and Stanton Streets

We're asked not to think, like pansies do
That the pinnately compound, ovate, lanceolate, non-linear,
             lobed, compound, toothed, alternate, opposite,
                palmate, heart-shaped, stalkless, clasping,
                perfoliate, and basal rosette-ish leaves
Can heal like the comfrey
And cause to grow together
The rough hairy leaves of the city's people and
             the rough hairy leaves of the sublimity of
                a gardener's art
Made with vegetarian shit & free as cupid's darts

If all our eyes had the clarity of apples
In a world as altered
As if by the wood betony
And all kinds of basil were the only rulers of the land
It would be good to be together
Both under and above the ground
To be sane as the madwort,
Ripe as corn, safe as sage,
Various as dusty miller and hens & chickens,
In politics as kindly fierce and dragonlike as tarragon,
Revolutionary as the lily.

After Catullus and Horace

only the manners of centuries ago can teach me
how to address you my lover as who you are
O Sestius, how could you put up with my children
thinking all the while you were bearing me as in your mirror
it doesn't matter anymore if spring wreaks its fiery
or lamblike dawn on my new-found asceticism, some joke
I wouldn't sleep with you or any man if you paid me
and most of you poets don't have the cash anyway
so please rejoin your fraternal books forever
while you miss in your securest sleep Ms Rosy-fingered dawn
who might've been induced to digitalize a part of you
were it not for your self-induced revenge of undoneness
it's good to live without a refrigerator! why bother
to chill the handiwork of Ceres and of Demeter?
and of the lonesome Sappho, let's have it warm for now.

Sonnet

Swell is the attribute of leisure
Found dead in immaculate house
I walked by you I walked
right by you, she read me
The pretty good poem of my father
I can hear the pen click, the pen
Makes noise, I do have to finish my work
For money, let's count to six

And when at the beginning fo a story
You I thank the blank rectangle of that blue
Fire escape experiment, it's a color
You can see because darker in minutes
Ending sky then never met did not
if not of something done, then imitation

Leslie Scalapino

from New Time

not abandonment
The rib cage floating in the shock occurs later, not chronologically — so that concentrating one *at first* chooses a moon bounding floating — in sheets of puring rain, as that occurs. A man clothed in black in the black, sneaking as feet placed side-by-side, like a big fox carrying a stick that floats out horizontal on his shoulder (dragged behind) with his wild eyeballs seen — our (my) wild eyeballs catch in the black

We're running outside tearing after him like bats on the boards a line — in bare feet by torrents of pouring snow in the sky — rather than the moon as chosen bounding. As one's sole movement's

silk black iris that's chest/thorax lifted off (set down;
weighing) it doesn't come
from them — is lifted off breathing, outside of one —
that is, one — weighed: not in the air, it is in the air
thorax black silk iris not image, breathing — in the air, yet
weighed — weighed is it being lifted off
(the frame weighed), it in the air

black of night isn't dependent

they appear — there

recurring

cubicles, of only city, from high up where people live —
separated by a river with a vast meadow on either side, people
fishing at a far distance on it — unknown how one makes a living
or anything, as there are no connections, while there are
companies — people 'communicate' only to people

the physical body
is only on that
of cubicles

———————

having to be ground under, socially — for nothing — hit on,
as insignificant yet not to ridicule — being so, by them, when a
woman say is carried (by them) never ridiculed so it is not of one —
people don't hate everyone. some while participating never did.

the physical body didn't
ever

———————

the place is always. what's coming is people attacking as sustaining their being in existence.

the one black oar parting the blue in fact — it is conditional on spring. I am.

bud — outside — but which is fully open — because outside of one as occurring lightly

a 'burst' that's away from one being returned to oneself — after one being away (outside). the outside is one's awareness

Why would they dismiss it because it's not the same?

It *exists* because it's not the same

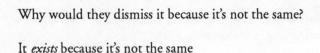

      running with bare feet, the snow falling, after the man
clothed in black in the black sky — is the neck cut out

      in their (other's) existence — one's neck cut out
      blossoms blossomed. in
time.

'Undermining' this, by seeing its appearance — places the individual doing so in the light of aberration (viewed by others, but also increasingly in the *act* of aberration by seeing (its) appearance) which may be regarded by a 'viewer' — as merely 'personal', not theoretical (which, as intepretive, assessment, is at that moment 'authority' itself)

if there's no overriding structure, "There is no character-simulacrum for it to reside in."

economic poverty (not being special) of them, one, is that being the physical body, *per se.* throughout.

which isn't inner.

from the waist — so that, turned the bulb that's oneself (thorax) — only — then — doesn't have any existence — turned (wherever one turns)

as conception — at waist of magnolia buds that exist in the day really

sewing the black silk irises — not when one turned at waist

sewing them, they have no shape literally except being that — from one's hand (being, in the air)

the irises only had existence in the black, before dawn, in fact

a man doesn't want me to become quiet again — go into ocean not weighed of before fighting — ever

formation of that of narrowed to no form in one — of black voluptuous lip — outside — voluptuous lips that (aren't) on black dawn, or before when it's black.

There was no intention — being done — with their existing.

not weighed before fighting which is the black, weighed, air — not the lips which have no weight — isn't following

if one's not contending ... so the inner isn't contending either...?

_____

After. Word

READERS STILL expect poetic forms to be stable, closed. Limited, self-limiting.

To a degree, the poets in this collection are attempting to open up closed systems of signification.

The problem for the reader is to find a meaningful way to read the texts which have been generated on different principles, which are multi- and non-linear, and which may be generated according to aleatory (chance) procedures.

These include working from "master" texts — history, law, theology, psychoanalysis, poetics, market reports — setting out from the source-texts, proceeding via combinations of "text randomizers," disordering the text at different levels — sentence clause phrase syllable grapheme — and other more purely lexical tactics of disarray.

Such procedures have been used by poets from the beginnings of written culture. Arguably the spatio-temporal difference now incurred is one precipitated by our imminence to "cybertextual technologies" of the future.[1]

For these texts to "work" for the reader demands active involvement but also recognition and acceptance that the texts are so structured. Attempts to read according to the procedures for a Shakespeare sonnet can clearly only produce frustration.

The relevance of the above to the procedures of many of these poets, who put their trust in "radical form",[2] is, despite the variables, critical. For trust in "radical form" implies openness to the challenge of meaning-generation wherever it may be accessed, and by whatever strategies — a form not handed down, but arrived at, one which the poet *discovers in and through the process of work* the

1 See John Cayley's "Beyond Codexspace, Potentialities of Literary Cybertext", due to be published in *Visible Language*, 1996, to whose ideas and the stimulation of his practice at the cutting edge of cybertechnology I am greatly indebted.
2 Edward Foster (in Preface, *Postmodern Poetry: The Talisman Interviews*, 1994).

logical extension of the inherent capabilities of the so-called "open-field" composition of earlier post-war American poetries such as those of Olson and Black Mountain.

Radical form implies "a truly radical politics that does not depend on a transcendent and ulterior authority". [3]

As well as aleatory experiment with different rule-set variables, we may employ deconstructive techniques, make use of "master-texts", as in Susan Howe's work, to critique the meaning of authority, the reading of history, to undertake a radical revision of both meaning and history, and of the hegemonic alliances that have excluded certain groups of actors — women, American Indians — from those histories, those lawbooks. These poets, like Howe, engaging *with* history, require the reader to call up dissimilar reading-processes from poets, who, to use Rosmarie Waldrop's phrase, are committed to exploring the "web of signs", whose primary interest is not in translating experience into writing, or whose will is directed towards the consummation, the dance of meaning-generation through attention to the linguistic/visual surface, through sound and performance.

Because the historically engaged poetic is, by definition, spatio-temporally engaged, the reader has fewer adjustments in content and value to make in reading procedures.

Leaving aside those poets whose methods are continuous with stable, transparent meaning, however poetically worked, whose use of artifice is in no determinate degree different from that of conventionally based or "traditional" poetries, there are clusters of language operated by some poets here which will not yield up meaning to the reader unless it is understood that the text has been worked upon to generate new meaning by exposing underlying generative linguistic structures. In other words, a radical swerve or deviation from traditional literary language-use has been employed, to subvert the rigid meanings that traditional structures produce.

To access these modes of operation the reader will need actively to enter into the procedures, and become a participant in discover-

3 Edward Foster, op cit.

ing the new meaning being generated. It follows that there is no final authority of the text, in the text, nor can there be any authoritative text in the sense of a stable, closed structure.

These comments clearly do not assist with all the poets in *Out of Everywhere*; they may help to point towards some of the goals aimed at, and the satisfactions to be expected.

To take as example, Carla Harryman's "After Theresa Hak Kyung Cha's *Dictée*" (from *Dimblue*) (page 49), where the reference in the title, while obscure, can be reached — references may be located, meanings supplied. The extract begins, "The arrogance of the contemporary in relationship to the contemporary. Water. A soft relationship...." And continues.

These ideas circling around history, the subject, literacy, operate at the level of phrase, syllable, morpheme and generally refuse the sentence or clause. The paradigm for this piece occurs in the interrogative word — "Child? Water? History?" — and curtailed trope, "as speaking child", in question, response and juxtaposition — "But leaves and water he it or she." The disarrangement of language at the surface level baulking expectation of ordered sequential thought allows multiple approaches to circle about the relationships between the contemporary, history, the subject, and the relationship between the human and other creation — "But leaves and water he it or she" — to be opened, brushed, to be further prised, teased in the continuing sequence. The note is always open — "Does delicious silence hear delicious silence written?"

The extract enacts protest against the closure of authoritative meaning. By the last section the circling units of language are moved in closer to known linguistic patterns:

"Although voices disappear as fast as the contemporary arrogance taken as history can obliterate them.... The child sings. And contradicts. She brings preference to history."

In conclusion, these notes are intended as pointing only, to hail potentially receptive readers, not to address cognoscenti. We seek through our labour to extend the challenge of reading writing that we believe in, precisely because it is still radical and resistant to cultural closure, where, to quote Cayley again, the "content-as-form is inherently protean ... shape-shifting ... radically indeterminate". In this view, to adapt Waldrop,[4] there is nothing before the Word. "We cannot get out of language. Only God can."

After [the] Word is silence. Where, depending on each reader, God is. Or is not.

Wendy Mulford

4 See interview between Edward Foster and Rosmarie Waldrop in *Postmodern Poetry: The Talisman Interviews*, op cit.

Bibliographies

RAE ARMANTROUT is the author of six books of poetry, most recently *Necromance* (Sun & Moon, 1991), *Couverture* (Les Cahiers de Royaumont, 1991) and *Made to Seem* (Sun & Moon, 1995). Her poems have appeared in several important anthologies, including *In the American Tree* (National Poetry Foundation, 1986), *Language Poetries* (New Directions, 1987), *Postmodern American Poetry* (Norton, 1994) and *From the Other Side of the Century: A New American Poetry 1960–1990* (Sun & Moon, 1994). Her critical essays have appeared in *American Literature*, *Poetics Journal* and *Sagetrieb*. She lives in San Diego, California, where she teaches in the literature department of the University of California.

CAROLINE BERGVALL is a poet and a performance writer. She has published texts in a number of magazines such as *Raddle Moon, Angel Exhaust, Fragmente, Trois*. She has developed performances and installations with other artists and was awarded the Showroom Live Art Commission 1993 for her choral poem *Strange Passage* (Equipage, 1993). Recent texts will also be featured in *Conductors of Chaos: The Picador Poets*. Currently a lecturer in Performance Writing at Dartington College of Arts.

NICOLE BROSSARD was born in Montreal, Quebec, in 1943 where she now lives. Poet, novelist and essayist, her books translated from the French into English include *A Book* (1976), *Daydream Mechanics* (1980), *Lovhers* (1986), *French Kiss* (1986), *The Aerial Letters* (1988) and *Picture Theory* (1990). In 1965, she co-founded the important literary journal *La Barre du Jour*. She was twice awarded Canada's most prestigious prize, the Governor General's Award for Poetry. She has also received Le Grand Prix de Poésie 1989 de la Fondation Les Forges. Her work has been translated into English, Italian and German.

PAULA CLAIRE has been performing her sound poetry, exhibiting her visual texts and collaborating with poets and musicians internationally since 1970. In 1978 she founded the International

Concrete Poetry Archive (ICPA), a collection of sound and visual poetry made by exchanging her work with exponents worldwide. In 1980 she established her own press, ICPA Publications, through which she publishes her own work and the work of other sound and visual poets. Numerous publications available, mainly from Writers Forum and ICPA, including *Declarations: Poems 1961–1991*, a comprehensive catalogue of her work with illustrations. She lives in Oxford.

TINA DARRAGH was born in Pittsburgh, Pennsylvania, in 1950. She attended Trinity College in Washington, DC, and continues to live in the Washington area with her husband, poet P Inman, and their son Jack. Tina earns her keep as a librarian. Publications include: *scale sliding* (Burning Deck, 1989), *a(gain)-st the odds* (Potes & Poets, 1989) and *adv. fans — the 1968 series* (Leave Books, 1993). Her poems have appeared in several important anthologies, including *The L=A=N=G=U=A=G=E Book* (Southern Illinois University Press, 1984), *In the American Tree* (National Poetry Foundation, 1986), *"Language" Poetries* (New Directions, 1987) and *From the Other Side of the Century: A New American Poetry 1960–1990* (Sun & Moon, 1994).

DEANNA FERGUSON was born in 1962 in Cranbrook, British Columbia. She is the author of five chapbooks including *Democratique* (1991) and *ddilemma* (1994), both from Cleave Press, and *The Relative Minor* (Tsunami Editions, 1993). She lives in Vancouver, BC, is a publisher of Tsunami Editions and an editor of *BOO Magazine*.

KATHLEEN FRASER is the author of 14 books of poetry, including *when new time folds up* (Chax Press, 1993) and *Wing* (Em Press, 1995). Her *Collected Poems (1964–1994)* is forthcoming from the National Poetry Foundation. During the eighties, she published and edited *HOW(ever)*, a journal focused on modernist and contemporary innovative practice in women's writing. She has just completed a book of essays and is translating work by Italian women poets. She lives in Rome and San Francisco. The poem series "Wing", excerpted here, was written in response to Mel

Bochner's *Drawings,* exhibited December 1988 at the David Nolan Gallery, New York, and to his 1993 installation, *Via Tasso,* in Rome at the Museo Storico della Liberazione di Roma.

BARBARA GUEST was a longtime resident of New York City, where she formed contacts with both poets and artists, collaborating with many artists and contributing critical writings to art journals. Author of numerous books, including the acclaimed biography of HD, *Herself Defined: HD the Poet and her World* (Doubleday, 1984). She has over a dozen books of poetry, including *Moscow Mansions* (Viking, 1973), *Fair Realism* (Sun & Moon, 1989) and *Defensive Rapture* (Sun & Moon, 1993). Her *Selected Poems* are due from Sun & Moon, to be followed by Carcanet in the UK. She now lives in Berkeley, California.

CARLA HARRYMAN is the author of *There Never Was a Rose Without a Thorn:* selected prose writings (City Lights, 1995), *Memory Play* (O Books, 1994), *In the Mode of* (Zasterle, 1991), *Animal Instincts:* prose, plays and essays (This, 1989), *Vice* (Potes & Poets, 1987), *The Middle* (Gaz, 1983), *Property* (Tuumba, 1982), *Under the Bridge* (This, 1980) and *Percentage* (Tuumba, 1979). Her recent theatre works include a production of *Memory Play* (The Lab, San Francisco, 1994) and a textual adaptation for Erling Wold's opera *A Little Girl Dreams of Taking the Veil,* based on the Max Ernst collage novel (Intersection, San Francisco, 1995).

LYN HEJINIAN was born in 1941 and lives in California. She is the co-editor and publisher (with Barrett Watten) of *Poetics Journal.* Numerous collections of her writing include *Writing is an Aid to Memory* (The Figures, 1978), *My Life* (Burning Deck, 1980, revised Sun & Moon, 1987), *Oxota: A Short Russian Novel* (The Figures, 1991), *The Cell* (Sun & Moon, 1992) and *The Cold of Poetry* (Sun & Moon, 1994). *Description* (1990) and *Xenia* (1994), her translations from the work of contemporary Russian poet Arakdii Dragomoschchenko, have also been published by Sun & Moon. She is a member of the Poetics faculty at New College, California, and also a lecturer in the University of California.

FANNY HOWE teaches at the University of California, San Diego, and is a mother of three. She has published several books of fiction and of poetry. Some of these are *Forty Whacks* (1969), *First Marriage* (1975), *Bronte Wilde* (1976), *Famous Questions* (1989), *The Lives of a Spirit* (1986), *In the Middle of Nowhere* (1984), *Poem from a Single Pallet* (1981), *Introduction to the World* (1985), *Robeson Street* (1985), *The Vineyard* (1988), *The End* (1992) and *O'Clock,* her first UK publication, from Reality Street Editions (1995).

SUSAN HOWE is a poet and Professor of English at the State University of New York at Buffalo. She is the author of numerous critical essays including *My Emily Dickinson* (North Atlantic Books, 1985) and *The Birth-Mark: Unsettling the Wilderness in American Literary History* (Wesleyan University Press, 1993). Her many books of poetry include *Singularities* (Wesleyan University Press, 1990), *The Europe of Trusts: Selected Poems* (Sun & Moon, 1990) and *The Nonconformist's Memorial* (New Directions, 1993). A long essay on the film-maker Chris Marker will be included in *Beyond Document: The Art of Non-Fiction Film* (Wesleyan University Press, 1995) and *I my Early Poems* is forthcoming from New Directions, 1996.

GRACE LAKE was born in 1948. Poems have appeared in many magazines and in the pamphlets *La Facciata* (Poetical Histories, 1989), *viola tricolor* (1993) and *Bernache Nonnette* (1995), both from Equipage, Cambridge.

KAREN MAC CORMACK was born in Zambia. She lives in Toronto where she subscribes to British and Canadian citizenship. She is the author of five books of poetry, including *Straw Cupid* (Nightwood Editions, 1987), *Quirks and Quillets* (Chax Press, 1991), *Marine Snow* (*ECW Press,* 1995); *The Tongue Moves Talk* (Chax Press) is forthcoming in 1996. Her work has appeared most recently in the anthologies *The Art of Practice: Forty-Five Contemporary Poets* (Potes & Poets, 1994), *The Last Word* (Insomniac Press, 1995) and *The Gertrude Stein Awards in Innovative Writing 1993–1994* (Sun & Moon).

BERNADETTE MAYER has been involved in the New York City poetry community for many years. She served as director of the Poetry Project at St Mark's Church from 1980–84 and since then has led numerous writing workshops at the project and at The New School for Social Research. She has published 15 books of poetry and prose, most recently *The Formal Field of Kissing* (Tender Buttons Press, 1990), *A Bernadette Mayer Reader* (New Directions, 1992) and *The Desires of Mothers to Please Others in Letters* (Hard Press, 1994).

GERALDINE MONK is a poet and performance artist whose work is represented in many anthologies. Her numerous publications include *Walks in a Daisy Chain* (Magenta, 1991), *The Sway of Precious Demons: Selected Poems* (North & South, 1992) and *Interregnum* (Creation Books, 1994), which was described as "an exhilarating flux of human-animal-alien corporealities ... eerie, violent Burroughsian". She is currently working on the performance of *Hidden Cities*, commissioned by The Ruskin School of Fine Art, Oxford University.

WENDY MULFORD started the Cambridge-based Street Editions in 1972 which recently merged with Ken Edwards' Reality Studios to become Reality Street Editions. She is the author of several collections of poetry including *Bravo to Girls and Heroes* (Street Editions, 1977), *Late Spring Next Year: Poems 1979–86* (Loxwood Stoneleigh, 1987), *The ABC of Writing* (Torque Press, 1985) and *The Bay of Naples* (Reality Studios, 1992). She is the co-editor of *The Virago Book of Love Poetry* (1990). Her prose includes *This Narrow Place: Sylvia Townsend Warner and Valentine Ackland* (Pandora, 1988). Recent work in *Exact Change Yearbook* (1995) and *The East Anglian Sequence*, forthcoming from Spectacular Diseases.

MELANIE NEILSON was born in Tennessee and grew up in San Diego, California. She lives in Brooklyn with her husband, Brandt Junceau. Her work is featured in the anthologies *Writing from the New Coast* (SUNY, Buffalo, with o-blek, 1994) and *The Art of Practice* (Potes & Poets, 1994). She is the co-editor, with Jessica

Grim, of *Big Allis*. Her books include *Civil Noir* (Roof Books, 1991) and *Prop and Guide* (The Figures, 1991). *Album* is forthcoming from Potes & Poets in 1995.

MAGGIE O'SULLIVAN, poet, performer, artist, publisher. Recent anthologies include *50: A Celebration of Sun & Moon Classics* (Sun & Moon, 1995), *Verbi Visi Voco: A Performance of Poetry* (Writers Forum, 1992) and *Floating Capital* (Potes & Poets, 1991). Among her eleven published poetic works are *A Natural History in 3 Incomplete Parts* from her own press, Magenta (1985), *Unofficial Word* (Galloping Dog, 1988), *In the House of the Shaman* (Reality Street Editions, 1993) and *Excla,* a collaboration with Bruce Andrews (Writers Forum, 1993). *Palace of Reptiles* is forthcoming from Sun & Moon in 1996.

CARLYLE REEDY is a poet best known for her multimedia theatre and performance art works. Her poetry is featured in the anthologies *Children of Albion* (Penguin, 1969), *Matières d'Angleterre* (1984) and *The Virago Book of Love Poetry* (1990), and *Poets on Writing: Britain 1970–1991* (Macmillan, 1992) carries an essay on some of her work. Among her publications are *Sculpted in This World* (Bluff Books, 1979) and *The Orange Notebook* (Reality Studios, 1984). *Obituaries & Celebrations* is due to appear from Words Worth Press.

JOAN RETALLACK has been active in performance and visual arts and is the author of five books of poetry and numerous critical essays on experimental poetry and poetics as well as her recent *MUSICAGE/CAGE MUSES on Words. Art. Music: John Cage in Conversation with Joan Retallack* (Wesleyan University Press, 1995). Her poetry has appeared in many anthologies including *From the Other Side of the Century: A New American Poetry 1960–1990* (Sun & Moon, 1994) and *The Art of Practice: 45 Contemporary Poets* (Potes & Poets, 1994). Among her poetry books are *Errata 5uite* (Edge Books, 1993), *WESTERN CIV CONT'D* (Pyramid Atlantic, 1995) and *AFTERRIMAGES* (Wesleyan University Press, 1995). She lives in the Washington DC area.

DENISE RILEY was born in Carlisle in 1948. She lives in London with her three children, working at Goldsmiths' College, and as an editor. Her prose books are *War in the Nursery* (Virago, 1983) and *"Am I That Name?" Feminism and the Category of "Women" in History* (Macmillan, 1988). She edited *Poets on Writing: Britain 1970–1991* (Macmillan, 1992) and is writing about social philosophies from 1880 to 1917. She's published several collections of poetry, including *Marxism for Infants* (Street Editions, 1977), *Dry Air* (Virago, 1985) and *Mop Mop Georgette* (Reality Street Editions, 1993).

LISA ROBERTSON edits *Raddle Moon*, with Susan Clark and Catriona Strang. Her work has been included in the anthologies *Exact Change Yearbook* and *Gertrude Stein Awards in Innovative American (sic) Poetry 1993–1994* (Sun & Moon). Her books are *The Badge* (Berkeley Horse, 1994), *The Apothecary* (Tsunami, 1991) and *XEclogue* (Tsunami, 1993). Occasional art critic.

LESLIE SCALAPINO lives in Oakland, California, and is the author of many books of prose, essays and plays, including *Defoe* (Sun & Moon, 1994) and *How Phenomena Appear to Unfold* (Potes & Poets, 1991). Her poetic plays have been performed by the Poets Theatre in San Francisco and Los Angeles and the Eye and Ear Theatre in New York. These include *Or* and *At Dawn* (1989) and *Goya's LA* (1994). Her poetry is included in many journals and anthologies including *From the Other Side of the Century: A New American Poetry 1960–1990* (Sun & Moon, 1994). Among her many books of poetry are *Considering how exaggerated music is* (North Point Press, 1982) and *Crowd and not evening or light* (O Books/Sun & Moon, 1992). She is also the editor, designer and publisher of O Books, a poetry press with more than 30 titles.

CATRIONA STRANG is a co-editor of *Barscheit* and *Raddle Moon* and the author of *Low Fancy*, a book-length translation of the Carmina Burana (ECW Press, 1993), *The Barscheit Horse*, a collaborative chapbook with Christine Stewart and Lisa Robertson (The Berkeley Horse, 1993) and *TEM* (Barscheit, 1992). Her work has appeared in numerous magazines and in the anthology *Exact Change Yearbook*. She frequently collaborates with noted clarinetist and soprano saxophonist François Houle. She is currently working on a songbook with Nancy Shaw and Monika Gagnon.

FIONA TEMPLETON lives between New York and Scotland. Co-founder of London's Theatre of Mistakes, 1974–79. Performance works include: *YOU — The City*, an intimate city-wide play for an audience of one (1988 New York, 1989 London — published by Roof, 1990 — film just completed); *Recognition* (1994), a solo about mortality, artifice and relation; *Delirium of Interpretations*, an antibiographical play (1991 — published by Sun & Moon, 1995). *Cells of Release* was a time-based writing installation at an abandoned prison in Philadelphia, with Amnesty International. Other books: *London* (Sun & Moon, 1984); *Elements of Performance Art*, with Anthony Howell (Ting Books, 1976); *Hi Cowboy* (forthcoming from Pointing Device in the UK).

ROSMARIE WALDROP was born in Kitzingen, Germany, in 1935. She lives in Providence, RI, where she co-edits Burning Deck Press (with more than 155 titles of poetry and fiction) with Keith Waldrop. She is the author of numerous books of poetry, criticism and translation. *A Key Into the Language of America* is just out from New Directions. Other recent books of poems are *Lawn of Excluded Middle* (Tender Buttons, 1993) and *The Reproduction of Profiles* (New Directions, 1987). Station Hill has published her two novels: *The Hanky of Pippin's Daughter* (1987) and *A Form/ of Taking/ It All* (1990). She translates from French and German (Edmond Jabès, Jacques Roubaud, Paul Celan, Friederike Mayröcker, Elke Erb) and has recently been a guest of the DAAD Künstlerprogramm in Berlin.

DIANE WARD was born in 1956 in Washington, DC, and currently lives in Southern California with her husband and son. Her work has appeared in numerous periodicals and in the recent anthologies *Postmodern American Poetry* (Norton, 1994) and *From the Other Side of the Century: A New American Poetry 1960–1990*

(Sun & Moon, 1994). Her books include *Never Without One* (Roof Books, 1984), *Relation* (Roof Books, 1989) and *Imaginary Movie* (Potes & Poets, 1992). *World Ceiling* is forthcoming from Roof Books, 1995.

HANNAH WEINER was born in Providence, RI, in 1928 and graduated from Radcliffe College 1950. Began to write poetry in 1963. The words began to appear in 1972 and led to *Clairvoyant Journal*, a three-voice performance poetry book about learning, explaining instructions and the counter voice. Books include *Magritte Poems* (Poetry Newsletter, 1970), *Clairvoyant Journal* (United Artists, 1978), *Little Books/Indians* (Roof, 1980) and *Silent Teachers Remembered Sequel* (Tender Buttons, 1993). Her work exists on CD — *Live at the Gap*; video — *Clairvoyant Journal*; and cassettes — *Clairvoyant Journal* (New Wilderness), and *Weeks,* (Xeroxial Endarchy).

MARJORIE WELISH, a poet and art critic living in New York, has published four books of poems: *Handwritten* (Sun, 1979), a chapbook, *Two Poems* (Z Press, 1981), *The Windows Flew Open* (Burning Deck, 1991) and *Casting Sequences* (University of Georgia Press, 1993). Her work is in numerous anthologies including *A Postmodern American Poetry* (Norton, 1994), *The Gertrude Stein Awards in Innovative American Poetry* (Sun & Moon, 1994) and *From the Other Side of the Century: A New American Poetry 1960–1990* (Sun & Moon, 1994). An art critic since 1968, she has published extensively on modern and post-modern art for such publications as *Arts Magazine, Art Criticism, Bomb, Partisan Review* and *Salmagundi*. A catalogue essay on Robert Rauschenberg for the Modern Art Museum of Fort Worth, Texas, appeared in autumn 1995.

Postscript

WHEN REALITY Street Editions decided there was a need for an anthology to showcase work by women who, broadly speaking, were working with language — disordering and deconstructive techniques, at the leading edge of new poetics — we realised that we did not have the necessary time to undertake the considerable task of compilation.

We therefore invited Maggie O'Sullivan, who works in a linguistically-rich performative tradition, to edit the anthology, and gave her a free hand.

We are extremely grateful to Maggie for all her hard work, which has made possible the fulfilment of the project.

Inevitably, given the range and richness of the new writing, and even working within her brief which limited her to work by poets from the US, Canada and the UK, Maggie has been forced to make some hard choices. As with any anthology, a dozen different editors would have come up with as many different selections; in the end, no selection can be definitive, but we are confident that this one will point readers in fruitful directions.

Of those poets not represented here, the pioneering work of Anne Waldman, Diane di Prima and Alice Notley can certainly be taken as read; among the Americans and Canadians, Mei-mei Berssenbrugge, Rachel Blau Du Plessis, Abigail Child, Susan Clark, Norma Cole, Beverly Dahlen, Lydia Davis, Jean Day, Lynne Dreyer, Johanna Drucker, Susan Gevirtz, Erica Hunt, Sheila E Murphy, Laura Moriarty and Gail Sher are just some of the names that could have as easily been included, and there are many more whose work is only now beginning to be published. The range is smaller in the British Isles, but interested readers of this book should certainly seek out the work of Helen Kidd, Frances Presley, Elaine Randell, Hazel Smith and Catherine Walsh; again, there are younger writers coming up.

In conclusion, the anthology does not, and cannot, aim to be more than a sampling, a fine tasting, of this writing. We would draw readers' attention to the work by women and men being published by presses such as Burning Deck, Chax Press, Equipage, The Figures, North & South, O Books, Pig Press, Potes & Poets,

Roof Books, Spectacular Diseases, Sun & Moon, Tender Buttons and Writers Forum; and to poetry and theoretical writing in magazines such as *Active in Airtime, Angel Exhaust, Avec, Big Allis, Five Fingers Review, Fragmente, Object Permanence, Parataxis, Raddle Moon, Ribot* and *Talisman*.

Many of these publications are hard to find in mainstream bookshops, but can be ordered in North America from Small Press Distribution, 1814 San Pablo Avenue, Berkeley, CA 94702, USA, telephone 510-549-3336. In the UK, Compendium Bookshop (234 Camden High Street, London NW1, telephone 0171-267 1525) remains the best retail outlet for this kind of work; mail order suppliers specialising in this area are Paul Green (83b London Road, Peterborough, Cambs. PE2 9BS) and Peter Riley (27 Sturton Street, Cambridge CB1 2QG, telephone 01223-327 455).

Wendy Mulford, Ken Edwards
Publishers, Reality Street Editions

Other titles published by Reality Street Editions

Kelvin Corcoran: *Lyric Lyric*
Allen Fisher: *Dispossession and Cure*
Susan Gevirtz: *Taken Place*
Fanny Howe: *O'Clock*
Maggie O'Sullivan: *In the House of the Shaman*
Denise Riley: *Mop Mop Georgette*
Peter Riley: *Distant Points*
Sarah Kirsch: *T*

For further details and news of forthcoming publications, please write to either the London or Suffolk address, given on the reverse of the title page, or email 100344.2546@compuserve.com